PROFIT PLANNER

SUCCESS

Risks, hard work, late nights, struggles, failures, persistence, action, discipline, courage, doubts, change, early mornings, pushing through boundaries, breaking habits, criticism, disappointments, adversity, rejections, losses, sacrifices, moving beyond the comfort zone...
Exhilarating!

Profit Planner

Copyright © 2017 by KISStrategies for Business Inc.

All rights reserved. No part of this book may be reproduced in any manner without written permission except in the case of brief quotations included in critical articles and reviews. For information, please contact Nicole Clark at KISStrategies for Business Inc. by email at Nicole@KISStrategies.ca

ISBN-13: 978-1542819466
ISBN-10: 1542819466

First Edition, First Printing

IF FOUND, PLEASE RETURN TO:

_____

_____

_____

EMAIL:_____

2017

January
Sun	Mon	Tue	Wed	Thu	Fri	Sat
1	2	3	4	5	6	7
8	9	10	11	12	13	14
15	16	17	18	19	20	21
22	23	24	25	26	27	28
29	30	31				

February
Sun	Mon	Tue	Wed	Thu	Fri	Sat
			1	2	3	4
5	6	7	8	9	10	11
12	13	14	15	16	17	18
19	20	21	22	23	24	25
26	27	28				

March
Sun	Mon	Tue	Wed	Thu	Fri	Sat
			1	2	3	4
5	6	7	8	9	10	11
12	13	14	15	16	17	18
19	20	21	22	23	24	25
26	27	28	29	30	31	

April
Sun	Mon	Tue	Wed	Thu	Fri	Sat
						1
2	3	4	5	6	7	8
9	10	11	12	13	14	15
16	17	18	19	20	21	22
23	24	25	26	27	28	29
30						

May
Sun	Mon	Tue	Wed	Thu	Fri	Sat
	1	2	3	4	5	6
7	8	9	10	11	12	13
14	15	16	17	18	19	20
21	22	23	24	25	26	27
28	29	30	31			

June
Sun	Mon	Tue	Wed	Thu	Fri	Sat
				1	2	3
4	5	6	7	8	9	10
11	12	13	14	15	16	17
18	19	20	21	22	23	24
25	26	27	28	29	30	

July
Sun	Mon	Tue	Wed	Thu	Fri	Sat
						1
2	3	4	5	6	7	8
9	10	11	12	13	14	15
16	17	18	19	20	21	22
23	24	25	26	27	28	29
30	31					

August
Sun	Mon	Tue	Wed	Thu	Fri	Sat
		1	2	3	4	5
6	7	8	9	10	11	12
13	14	15	16	17	18	19
20	21	22	23	24	25	26
27	28	29	30	31		

September
Sun	Mon	Tue	Wed	Thu	Fri	Sat
					1	2
3	4	5	6	7	8	9
10	11	12	13	14	15	16
17	18	19	20	21	22	23
24	25	26	27	28	29	30

October
Sun	Mon	Tue	Wed	Thu	Fri	Sat
1	2	3	4	5	6	7
8	9	10	11	12	13	14
15	16	17	18	19	20	21
22	23	24	25	26	27	28
29	30	31				

November
Sun	Mon	Tue	Wed	Thu	Fri	Sat
			1	2	3	4
5	6	7	8	9	10	11
12	13	14	15	16	17	18
19	20	21	22	23	24	25
26	27	28	29	30		

December
Sun	Mon	Tue	Wed	Thu	Fri	Sat
					1	2
3	4	5	6	7	8	9
10	11	12	13	14	15	16
17	18	19	20	21	22	23
24	25	26	27	28	29	30
31						

2018

January
Sun	Mon	Tue	Wed	Thu	Fri	Sat
31	1	2	3	4	5	6
7	8	9	10	11	12	13
14	15	16	17	18	19	20
21	22	23	24	25	26	27
28	29	30	31	1	2	3
4	5	6	7	8	9	10

February
Sun	Mon	Tue	Wed	Thu	Fri	Sat
28	29	30	31	1	2	3
4	5	6	7	8	9	10
11	12	13	14	15	16	17
18	19	20	21	22	23	24
25	26	27	28	1	2	3
4	5	6	7	8	9	10

March
Sun	Mon	Tue	Wed	Thu	Fri	Sat
25	26	27	28	1	2	3
4	5	6	7	8	9	10
11	12	13	14	15	16	17
18	19	20	21	22	23	24
25	26	27	28	29	30	31
1	2	3	4	5	6	7

April
Sun	Mon	Tue	Wed	Thu	Fri	Sat
1	2	3	4	5	6	7
8	9	10	11	12	13	14
15	16	17	18	19	20	21
22	23	24	25	26	27	28
29	30	1	2	3	4	5
6	7	8	9	10	11	12

May
Sun	Mon	Tue	Wed	Thu	Fri	Sat
29	30	1	2	3	4	5
6	7	8	9	10	11	12
13	14	15	16	17	18	19
20	21	22	23	24	25	26
27	28	29	30	31	1	2
3	4	5	6	7	8	9

June
Sun	Mon	Tue	Wed	Thu	Fri	Sat
27	28	29	30	31	1	2
3	4	5	6	7	8	9
10	11	12	13	14	15	16
17	18	19	20	21	22	23
24	25	26	27	28	29	30
1	2	3	4	5	6	7

July
Sun	Mon	Tue	Wed	Thu	Fri	Sat
1	2	3	4	5	6	7
8	9	10	11	12	13	14
15	16	17	18	19	20	21
22	23	24	25	26	27	28
29	30	31	1	2	3	4
5	6	7	8	9	10	11

August
Sun	Mon	Tue	Wed	Thu	Fri	Sat
29	30	31	1	2	3	4
5	6	7	8	9	10	11
12	13	14	15	16	17	18
19	20	21	22	23	24	25
26	27	28	29	30	31	1
2	3	4	5	6	7	8

September
Sun	Mon	Tue	Wed	Thu	Fri	Sat
26	27	28	29	30	31	1
2	3	4	5	6	7	8
9	10	11	12	13	14	15
16	17	18	19	20	21	22
23	24	25	26	27	28	29
30	1	2	3	4	5	6

October
Sun	Mon	Tue	Wed	Thu	Fri	Sat
30	1	2	3	4	5	6
7	8	9	10	11	12	13
14	15	16	17	18	19	20
21	22	23	24	25	26	27
28	29	30	31	1	2	3
4	5	6	7	8	9	10

November
Sun	Mon	Tue	Wed	Thu	Fri	Sat
28	29	30	31	1	2	3
4	5	6	7	8	9	10
11	12	13	14	15	16	17
18	19	20	21	22	23	24
25	26	27	28	29	30	1
2	3	4	5	6	7	8

December
Sun	Mon	Tue	Wed	Thu	Fri
25	26	27	28	29	
2	3	4	5		22
9	10	11		28	29
16	17				
23					

The 6 Pillars of Entrepreneurship

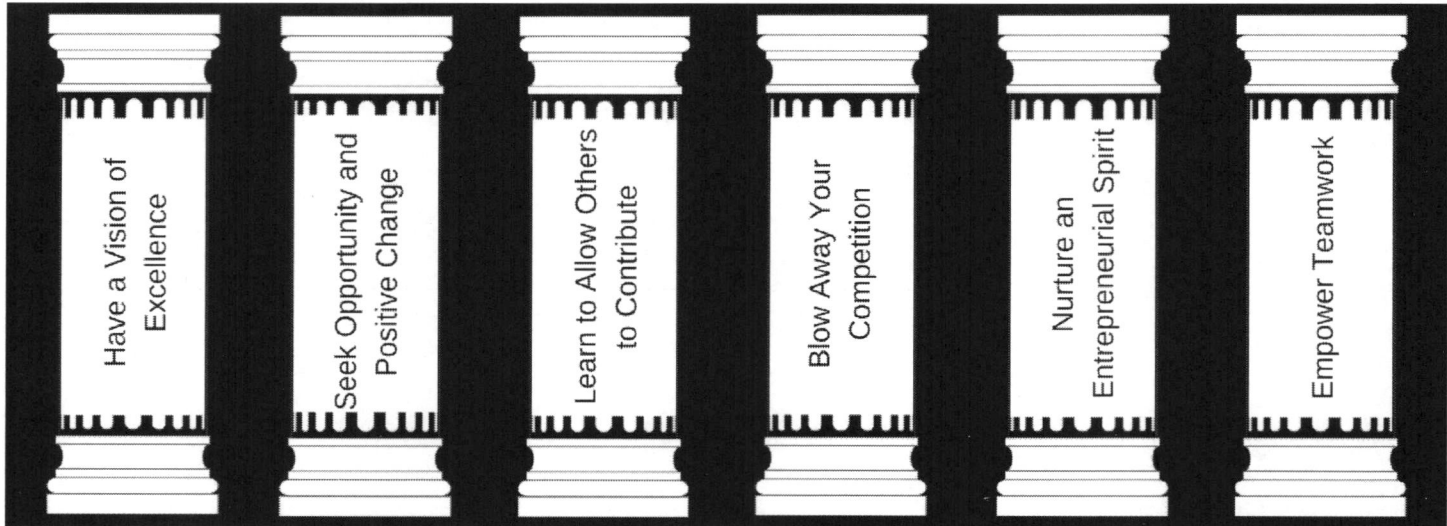

It is said that every entrepreneur owns a business, but not every business owner is an entrepreneur. Research shows that many businesses struggle to survive and then improve during the first couple of years of start-up; then they hit a wall where everything seems to plateau or even start declining. How can you avoid this wall in your business? Adopt the 6 Pillars of Entrepreneurship.

1. Have a Vision of Excellence - what is the better world you envision as a result of your company being successful? This is a big, bold statement - bigger than you and bigger than your company. What is the role of your company in this big, bold vision? What do you do? Why do you do it? Who do you do it for? How do you do it? Communicate this vision with all stakeholders in your company - shareholders, managers, staff, investors, lenders, suppliers.

2. Seek Opportunity and Positive Change - an opportunity has four anchors. It creates and/or adds value to your customer, it solves a problem or meets a need, it is a good fit with you and your business, and it has an opportunity for profit. Be open to change as it can create opportunities. Learn how to recognize an opportunity when it arises, or start creating your own opportunities.

3. Learn to Allow Others to Contribute - often as we launch our business, we take responsibility for doing everything within the business, from sales to bookkeeping to social media. At some point we need to give up the reins on controlling all the pieces in our business so we can get back to the fun of being an entrepreneur. Learn to trust others to make a contribution to your business.

4. Blow Away Your Competition - create a customer-centric climate in your business, continuously exceed expectations, ask for feedback from your customers on what is important to them and then deliver on it.

5. Nurture an Entrepreneurial Spirit - create an environment where everyone is encouraged to seek and communicate opportunities for your business. Whether this is a new product or service, or a more efficient way to accomplish something, or a way of cutting costs.

6. Empower Teamwork - It has long been recognized that teamwork is essential in the success of any organization, whether it is your business or your local hockey team. Developing a culture of teamwork encourages everyone to feel free to express their ideas as you all work together towards a common goal. You will also find people jumping in to help their colleagues when a hand is needed to complete a task or project.

Your Year with your Profit Planner, please complete the following 6 pages

can set BIG GOALS for your business for the next 12 months.

In order to **Rock Your Year**, you have to start by setting yourself up for success. If you are like most people, you have a large number of things that you would like to accomplish in your lifetime. It is important that you get all of these things out of your mind and onto paper. This exercise is also very useful in overcoming overwhelm. So, as a first step, do a Brain Dump. Write down absolutely everything that you want to do or need to do. Try to do this without judgement, without "I'll never be able to do that" or "Who do I think I am kidding?" Just keep writing until your mind cannot come up with anything more to write.

Use the space on this and the next page to do your Brain Dump. Feel free to add additional pages if needed.

> "Time is the coin of your life. It is the only coin you have, and only you can determine how it will be spent. Be careful lest you let other people spend it for you. "
> Carl Sandburg~

Now that you have completed your Brain Dump, you will probably notice that there are some bigger categories that encompass a number of items on your list. Name these bigger "Projects" and then list everything that goes with them. Perhaps one of the "Projects" is take a trip to Europe. Items under that project may include such things as book time off, research accommodations, book flight, phone travel agent and so on. Some of these items may also be able to be categorized, becoming objectives (Plan travel and accommodations) with action items beneath them. Now you have a big "Project" or Goal, objectives to help you accomplish it, and the action items that will get you there.

Move your items from your Brain Dump into either a Project, Objectives to complete the Project, or Action Items to help you reach those objectives.

Project 1:

Objective 1:		
Action Items:	1.	2.
3.	4.	5.
6.	7.	8.

Objective 2:		
Action Items:	1.	2.
3.	4.	5.
6.	7.	8.

Objective 3:		
Action Items:	1.	2.
3.	4.	5.
6.	7.	8.

Objective 4:		
Action Items:	1.	2.
3.	4.	5.
6.	7.	8.

Project 2:

Objective 1:		
Action Items:	1.	2.
3.	4.	5.
6.	7.	8.

Objective 2:		
Action Items:	1.	2.
3.	4.	5.
6.	7.	8.

Objective 3:		
Action Items:	1.	2.
3.	4.	5.
6.	7.	8.

Objective 4:		
Action Items:	1.	2.
3.	4.	5.
6.	7.	8.

Objective 5:		
Action Items:	1.	2.
3.	4.	5.
6.	7.	8.

Objective 6:		
Action Items:	1.	2.
3.	4.	5.
6.	7.	8.

Project 3:

Objective 1:		
Action Items:	1.	2.
3.	4.	5.
6.	7.	8.
Objective 2:		
Action Items:	1.	2.
3.	4.	5.
6.	7.	8.
Objective 3:		
Action Items:	1.	2.
3.	4.	5.
6.	7.	8.
Objective 4:		
Action Items:	1.	2.
3.	4.	5.
6.	7.	8.
Objective 5:		
Action Items:	1.	2.
3.	4.	5.
6.	7.	8.
Objective 6:		
Action Items:	1.	2.
3.	4.	5.
6.	7.	8.

Project 4:

Objective 1:		
Action Items:	1.	2.
3.	4.	5.
6.	7.	8.

Objective 2:		
Action Items:	1.	2.
3.	4.	5.
6.	7.	8.

Objective 3:		
Action Items:	1.	2.
3.	4.	5.
6.	7.	8.

Objective 4:		
Action Items:	1.	2.
3.	4.	5.
6.	7.	8.

Objective 5:		
Action Items:	1.	2.
3.	4.	5.
6.	7.	8.

Objective 6:		
Action Items:	1.	2.
3.	4.	5.
6.	7.	8.

> ## "Failing to plan is like planning to fail."
> ## ~ *Benjamin Franklin*

Now that you have organized your thoughts, it is time to set up to four **BIG GOALS** for the year ahead. The question is, what do you want to accomplish in the next 365 days? Choose **BIG GOALS** that, if you were to accomplish them, you would feel like you had had an extremely successful year. Make sure you use the SMART method of goal-setting to give you a 90% better chance at accomplishing your goals.

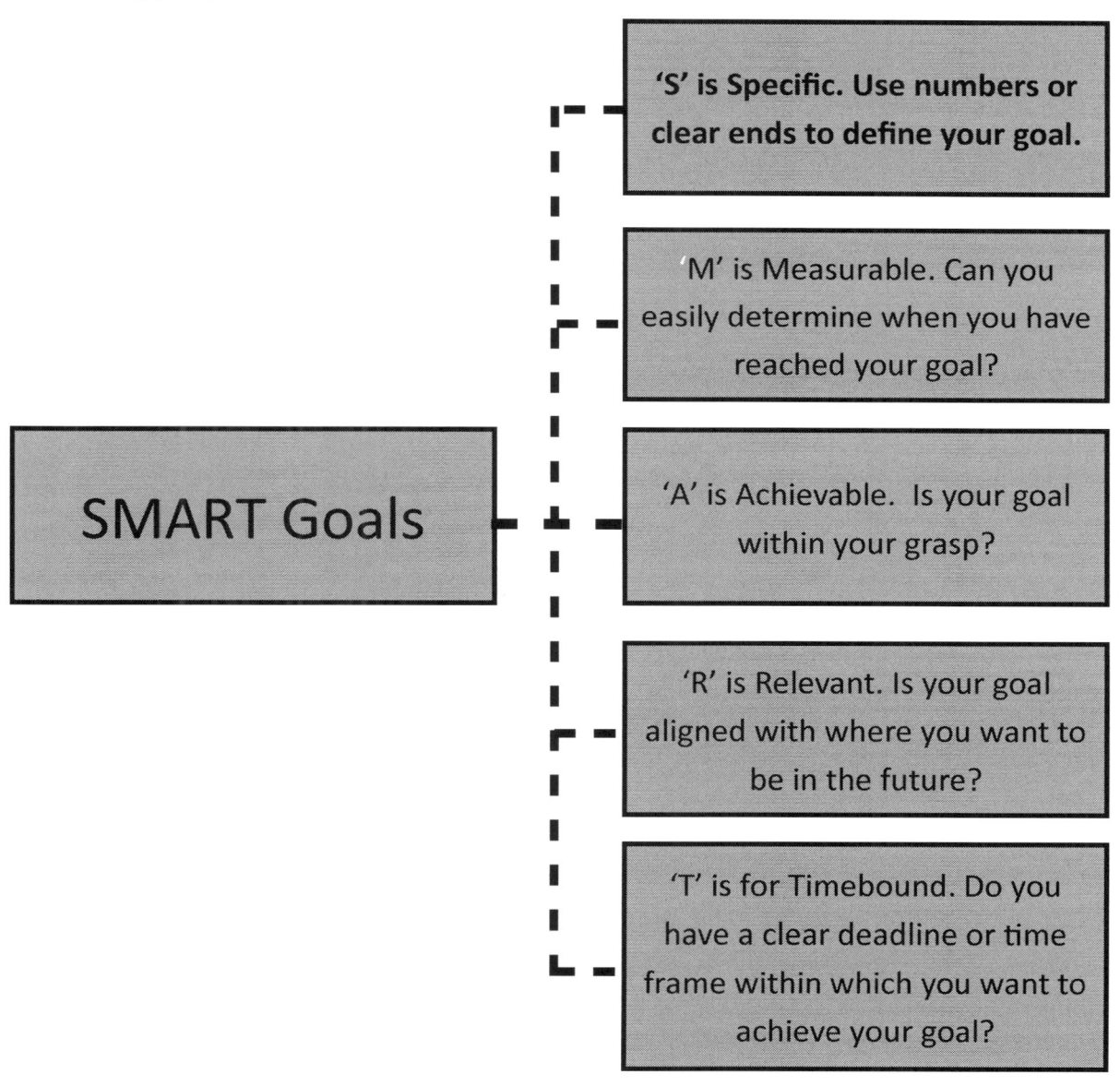

My Big Goals:

1. **To**

   by

2. **To**

   by

3. **To**

   by

4. **To**

   by

Now that you have your Big Goals, create monthly Objectives, which, by accomplishing them will lead to your achieving your Big Goals.

Month 1	
Month 2	
Month 3	
Month 4	
Month 5	
Month 6	
Month 7	
Month 8	
Month 9	
Month 10	
Month 11	
Month 12	

By chunking your goal down in this way it is easier to see that the Big Goal is reasonable and can be accomplished within the year.

Each week in your **Profit Planner** includes four pages to allow you to maximize your productivity and reach your goals for your business.

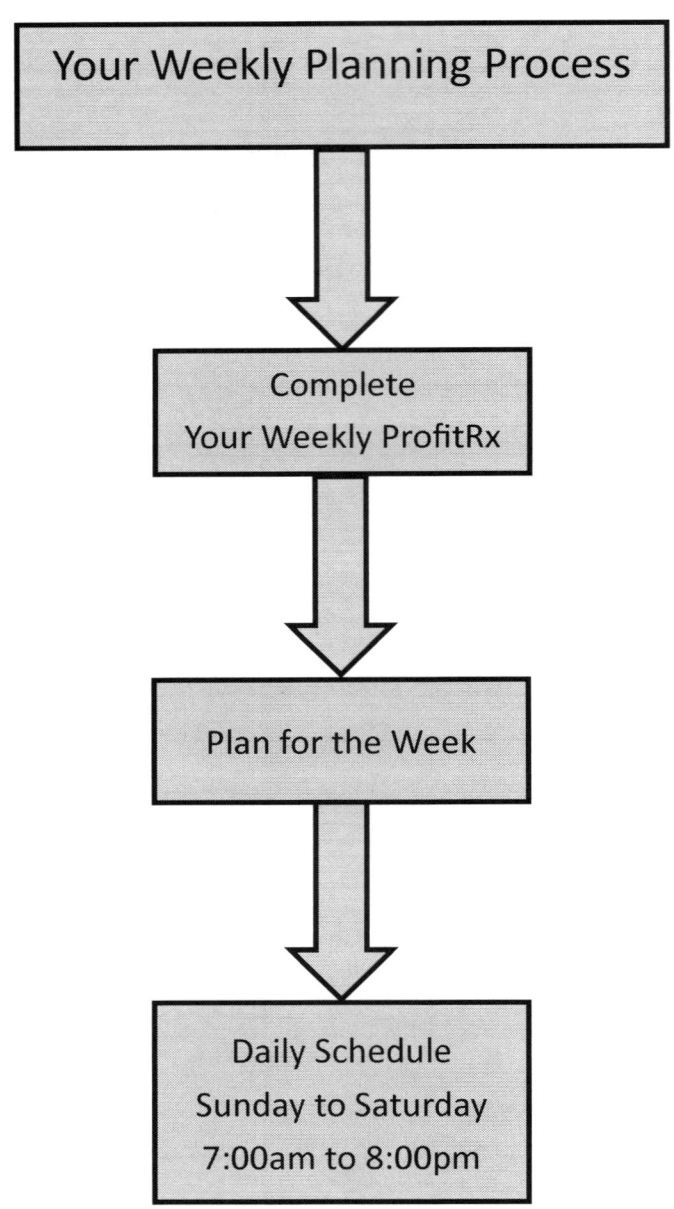

Your Weekly ProfitRx
Instructions

Your Weekly ProfitRx is a little bit of increasing the vibration of your energy and a lot about action. Have you ever noticed that when you put your energy into something productive that is in the direction of your goals, you get results? Not necessarily from the actions you were taking, often from a completely different direction. Put this into your weekly practice, and your results are sure to improve even if you are already accomplishing what you planned. Better yet, incorporate it into a daily practice. Send me an email at info@KISStrategies.ca and I will send you the template.

1. The evidence of my alignment with more profit last week was: Write down 5 proofs. These do not have to be big proofs; they could be as simple as
   - I got 10 new likes on my Facebook page
   - I paid my phone bill yesterday
   - I had a new client appointment
   - My sales this week were 10% higher than last week

2. This week I appreciate my business because: Write a couple of sentences or use point form to outline the things you appreciate. For example, I am so grateful that my business is opening doors to new opportunities. Yesterday at a networking event someone asked me to collaborate on a teleseminar which is something I have been wanting to do.

3. I choose to feel _____ about my business this week: Write a word or two that describes how you want to feel this week. For example, Excited, Get it Done, Fulfilled, Grateful

4. I am trusting my instincts by choosing these inspired actions to do this week. Write 1 to 3 inspired actions you will take this week. For example, commit to attending a particular workshop or seminar series by registering for it; finish reading a business book; start an important project I have been putting off because it is out of my comfort zone. These should somehow take you closer to reaching your business goals.

5. I trust the Universe to handle everything else I need to attract more profit: This is where you will write down something you are struggling with or seeking answers about. For example, as a business trainer, I have written "Content for my new workshop flows to me easily".

6. I would be blown away if this happened in my business: Without judgement as to how likely it is to happen, and without attachment as to whether or not it happens, write down something outrageous that you would like to have happen. For example, one of my clients wrote that one of her "bad debt" clients came by her office and paid off his debt to her company that was 3 years old. A completely different person came by and said his deceased brother had been a client 3 years earlier and he had just come across the outstanding invoice for $3,500. He paid it in full.

7. You won't believe when I tell you the amazing thing that happened in my business: Write a few sentences about the amazing results you are getting as if they had already happened. Again this should be written without judgement, meaning don't have any doubts about the outcome—don't think "I will never be able to do this" or "who am I trying to fool".

The Pareto Principle

20% of the Effort

Yields

80% of the Results

Originally the Pareto Principle arose from Vifredo Pareto's observation that % of Italians held 80% of the wealth of Italy. More generally, the Pareto Principle is the observation that **most things in life are not distributed evenly**. It can mean all of the following things:

- % of the workers produce 80% of the result
- % of the hockey players score 80% of the goals
- % of the volunteers in an organization do 80% of the work
- % of the customers create 80% of the revenue
- % of the input creates 80% of the result
- *% of your activities will yield 80% of your results*

If % of your work is driving 80% of your results, what systems can you put in place so you do less of the 80% and more of the %?

It may be that you read emails as they pop up on your computer and deal with them. Every time this happens you become distracted and, a University of California, Irvine study showed that an average office worker gets only 11 minutes on a task before they are distracted and it takes them minutes to get back to the task they were working on. Clearly, some new strategies are in order.

What might these strategies look like?

- Check and deal with your email twice per day, for an hour in the morning and an hour in the afternoon. Try to keep your Inbox at zero by answering, archiving and deleting emails.
- Block social media sites from the start of your day until your break and then from your break until the end of your day.
- Set aside two 3-hour time blocks per week during which you will take meetings. If it doesn't fit in with the other person's schedule, push it to the following week.

The following apps are just a few of the many available to help you attain better attention and focus (Google productivity apps for more):

1. Freedom - internet, social media and app blocker that works on your iPhone, iPad, Mac and Windows computers
2. Focus Booster - based on the Pomodoro technique for time-management, this app breaks down your work into minute sessions with a 5-minute break between each session.
3. Self-Control - if you need extra self-discipline, this app won't let you out of predetermined timed sessions even if you reboot your computer
4. Time Out - For the workaholics out there, Time Out reminds you to take a break by gently dimming the screen and showing you a message. You can take normal breaks (10 minutes after 50 minutes of work) or micro breaks (short pauses of 10 seconds every 10 minutes if you're really doing something stressful). Once the break is over, your screen fades back in, and you can get back to work.

Setting Weekly Goals for Each Month

Now that you have set your monthly goals and established strategies to maximize your time so that you are focussed on your % of productive tasks, it is time to chunk down those monthly objectives into weekly action steps. If you plan this now, you will find that you have created a detailed road map for accomplishing your Big Goals!

Doing Your Weekly Planning

Set aside minutes at the end of each week to do your weekly planning. Your weekly planning sheet looks like this and is included throughout your **Profit Planner**

For the week of	January 1 - 7,
Big Goal	To save up for and book a three week holiday in Hawaii to begin on Feb 5,
This Month's Objective	To research all costs associated with the trip.
This Week's Action Step	Identify the best travel agent in town and book an appointment to meet with them
This Week's Big Rocks	
Monday	Reach out to friends and family for a referral to a great travel agent
Tuesday	Do online research on Facebook, Yelp, and TripAdvisor to check ratings and reviews
Wednesday	Select travel agent and make appointment for meeting
Thursday	Reconfirm meeting with travel agent
Friday	Meet with travel agent
Additional Projects and Tasks for this Week	Finish content creation for Business Plan Development Workshop workbook
	Start research to determine what the topic of the next workshop should be
	Do data entry in CRM for week
	Follow-up with 5 potential clients
	Buy birthday gift for Mom

The point of using this format is that the tasks that are directly related to your Big Goal are given priority. We all, of course, have many other things to accomplish every week which is why we have made room for "Additional Projects and Tasks". It is important that you get your goal related tasks done first; this is your best chance of achieving the Big Goals you have set. At the end of the year, if you don't achieve your goal, it won't be for a lack of action on your part.

Daily Planning for Success

Do you own your day or does your day own you?

You can do all of the yearly, monthly and weekly planning you want, but if you don't have a plan for each day, you're screwed. Here is how we will plan our day throughout this planner.

Big Goal	To save up for and book a three week holiday in Hawaii to begin on February 5, 2018
This Month's Objective	To research all costs associated with the trip.
This Week's Action Step	Identify the best travel agent in town and book an appointment to meet with them
Today's Big Rock	Reach out to friends and family for a referral to a great travel agent
Today's Priority Tasks	
1.	Follow-up with 5 potential clients
2.	Finish content creation for Market Research section of BPD Workshop
Daily Tasks	
1.	Finish with Inbox at zero
2.	Return all voice mails
Today's Bonuses	
1.	Date night with hubby
2.	Yoga class

"An entrepreneur is someone who jumps off a cliff and builds a plane on the way down."

~ Reid Hoffman

Here's to your Profitable Journey!

Your Weekly ProfitRx

The evidence of my alignment with profit last week was:

This week I appreciate my business because:

This week I choose to feel _____ about my business.

I am trusting my instincts by choosing these inspired actions to do this week:

I trust the Universe to handle everything else I need to attract more profit:

I would be absolutely blown away if this happened this week:

You won't believe it when I tell you what happened in my business. Listen to this:

For the week of	
Big Goal	
This Month's Objective	
This Week's Action Step	
This Week's Big Rocks	
Monday	
Tuesday	
Wednesday	
Thursday	
Friday	
Additional Projects and Tasks for this Week	

> "You have brains in your head. You have feet in your shoes. You can steer yourself any direction you choose. You're on your own. And you know what you know. And YOU are the one who'll decide where to go..."
> ~ *Dr. Seuss*

Big Goal			
This Month's Objective			
Week's Action Step			
	Sunday	Monday	Tuesday
Today's Big Rock			
Priority Tasks			
Daily Tasks			
Daily Bonuses			
NOTES	7	7	7
	8	8	8
	9	9	9
	10	10	10
	11	11	11
	12	12	12
	1	1	1
	2	2	2
	3	3	3
	4	4	4
	5	5	5
	6	6	6
	7	7	7
	8	8	8

Wednesday	Thursday	Friday	Saturday
7	7	7	7
8	8	8	8
9	9	9	9
10	10	10	10
11	11	11	11
12	12	12	12
1	1	1	1
2	2	2	2
3	3	3	3
4	4	4	4
5	5	5	5
6	6	6	6
7	7	7	7
8	8	8	8

Your Weekly ProfitRx

The evidence of my alignment with profit last week was:

This week I appreciate my business because:

This week I choose to feel _____ about my business.

I am trusting my instincts by choosing these inspired actions to do this week:

I trust the Universe to handle everything else I need to attract more profit:

I would be absolutely blown away if this happened this week:

You won't believe it when I tell you what happened in my business. Listen to this:

For the week of	
Big Goal	
This Month's Objective	
This Week's Action Step	
This Week's Big Rocks	
Monday	
Tuesday	
Wednesday	
Thursday	
Friday	
Additional Projects and Tasks for this Week	

"In every success story, you will find someone who has made a courageous decision."

~ Peter F. Drucker

		Sunday	Monday	Tuesday
Big Goal				
This Month's Objective				
Week's Action Step				
Today's Big Rock				
Priority Tasks				
Daily Tasks				
Daily Bonuses				
NOTES		7	7	7
		8	8	8
		9	9	9
		10	10	10
		11	11	11
		12	12	12
		1	1	1
		2	2	2
		3	3	3
		4	4	4
		5	5	5
		6	6	6
		7	7	7
		8	8	8

Wednesday	Thursday	Friday	Saturday
7	7	7	7
8	8	8	8
9	9	9	9
10	10	10	10
11	11	11	11
12	12	12	12
1	1	1	1
2	2	2	2
3	3	3	3
4	4	4	4
5	5	5	5
6	6	6	6
7	7	7	7
8	8	8	8

Your Weekly ProfitRx

The evidence of my alignment with profit last week was:

This week I appreciate my business because:

This week I choose to feel _____ about my business.

I am trusting my instincts by choosing these inspired actions to do this week:

I trust the Universe to handle everything else I need to attract more profit:

I would be absolutely blown away if this happened this week:

You won't believe it when I tell you what happened in my business. Listen to this:

For the week of	
Big Goal	
This Month's Objective	
This Week's Action Step	
This Week's Big Rocks	
Monday	
Tuesday	
Wednesday	
Thursday	
Friday	
Additional Projects and Tasks for this Week	

> *"Success is nothing more than a few simple disciplines, practiced every day."*
> *~ Jim Rohn*

	Sunday	Monday	Tuesday
Big Goal			
This Month's Objective			
Week's Action Step			
Today's Big Rock			
Priority Tasks			
Daily Tasks			
Daily Bonuses			
NOTES	7	7	7
	8	8	8
	9	9	9
	10	10	10
	11	11	11
	12	12	12
	1	1	1
	2	2	2
	3	3	3
	4	4	4
	5	5	5
	6	6	6
	7	7	7
	8	8	8

Wednesday	Thursday	Friday	Saturday
7	7	7	7
8	8	8	8
9	9	9	9
10	10	10	10
11	11	11	11
12	12	12	12
1	1	1	1
2	2	2	2
3	3	3	3
4	4	4	4
5	5	5	5
6	6	6	6
7	7	7	7
8	8	8	8

Your Weekly ProfitRx

The evidence of my alignment with profit last week was:

This week I appreciate my business because:

This week I choose to feel _____ about my business.

I am trusting my instincts by choosing these inspired actions to do this week:

I trust the Universe to handle everything else I need to attract more profit:

I would be absolutely blown away if this happened this week:

You won't believe it when I tell you what happened in my business. Listen to this:

For the week of	
Big Goal	
This Month's Objective	
This Week's Action Step	
This Week's Big Rocks	
Monday	
Tuesday	
Wednesday	
Thursday	
Friday	
Additional Projects and Tasks for this Week	

"Continuous learning is the minimum requirement for success in any field."

~ Dennis Waitley

Big Goal			
This Month's Objective			
Week's Action Step			
	Sunday	**Monday**	**Tuesday**
Today's Big Rock			
Priority Tasks			
Daily Tasks			
Daily Bonuses			
NOTES	7	7	7
	8	8	8
	9	9	9
	10	10	10
	11	11	11
	12	12	12
	1	1	1
	2	2	2
	3	3	3
	4	4	4
	5	5	5
	6	6	6
	7	7	7
Big Goal	8	8	8

Wednesday	Thursday	Friday	Saturday
7	7	7	7
8	8	8	8
9	9	9	9
10	10	10	10
11	11	11	11
12	12	12	12
1	1	1	1
2	2	2	2
3	3	3	3
4	4	4	4
5	5	5	5
6	6	6	6
7	7	7	7
8	8	8	8

Your Weekly ProfitRx

The evidence of my alignment with profit last week was:

This week I appreciate my business because:

This week I choose to feel _____ about my business.

I am trusting my instincts by choosing these inspired actions to do this week:

I trust the Universe to handle everything else I need to attract more profit:

I would be absolutely blown away if this happened this week:

You won't believe it when I tell you what happened in my business. Listen to this:

For the week of	
Big Goal	
This Month's Objective	
This Week's Action Step	
This Week's Big Rocks	
Monday	
Tuesday	
Wednesday	
Thursday	
Friday	
Additional Projects and Tasks for this Week	

> "Enthusiasm is the sparkle in your eyes, the swing in your gait, the grip of your hand and the irresistible surge of will and energy to execute your ideas."
>
> ~ *Henry Ford*

		Sunday	Monday	Tuesday
Big Goal				
This Month's Objective				
Week's Action Step				
Today's Big Rock				
Priority Tasks				
Daily Tasks				
Daily Bonuses				
NOTES		7	7	7
		8	8	8
		9	9	9
		10	10	10
		11	11	11
		12	12	12
		1	1	1
		2	2	2
		3	3	3
		4	4	4
		5	5	5
		6	6	6
		7	7	7
		8	8	8

Wednesday	Thursday	Friday	Saturday
7	7	7	7
8	8	8	8
9	9	9	9
10	10	10	10
11	11	11	11
12	12	12	12
1	1	1	1
2	2	2	2
3	3	3	3
4	4	4	4
5	5	5	5
6	6	6	6
7	7	7	7
8	8	8	8

Your Weekly ProfitRx

The evidence of my alignment with profit last week was:

This week I appreciate my business because:

This week I choose to feel _____ about my business.

I am trusting my instincts by choosing these inspired actions to do this week:

I trust the Universe to handle everything else I need to attract more profit:

I would be absolutely blown away if this happened this week:

You won't believe it when I tell you what happened in my business. Listen to this:

For the week of	
Big Goal	
This Month's Objective	
This Week's Action Step	
This Week's Big Rocks	
Monday	
Tuesday	
Wednesday	
Thursday	
Friday	
Additional Projects and Tasks for this Week	

> "Desire is the key to motivation, but it's determination and commitment to an unrelenting pursuit of your goal -- a commitment to excellence -- that will enable you to attain the success you seek."
> ~ *Mario Andretti*

Big Goal			
This Month's Objective			
Week's Action Step			
	Sunday	Monday	Tuesday
Today's Big Rock			
Priority Tasks			
Daily Tasks			
Daily Bonuses			
NOTES	7	7	7
	8	8	8
	9	9	9
	10	10	10
	11	11	11
	12	12	12
	1	1	1
	2	2	2
	3	3	3
	4	4	4
	5	5	5
	6	6	6
	7	7	7
Big Goal	8	8	8

Wednesday	Thursday	Friday	Saturday
7	7	7	7
8	8	8	8
9	9	9	9
10	10	10	10
11	11	11	11
12	12	12	12
1	1	1	1
2	2	2	2
3	3	3	3
4	4	4	4
5	5	5	5
6	6	6	6
7	7	7	7
8	8	8	8

Your Weekly ProfitRx

The evidence of my alignment with profit last week was:

This week I appreciate my business because:

This week I choose to feel _____ about my business.

I am trusting my instincts by choosing these inspired actions to do this week:

I trust the Universe to handle everything else I need to attract more profit:

I would be absolutely blown away if this happened this week:

You won't believe it when I tell you what happened in my business. Listen to this:

For the week of	
Big Goal	
This Month's Objective	
This Week's Action Step	
This Week's Big Rocks	
Monday	
Tuesday	
Wednesday	
Thursday	
Friday	
Additional Projects and Tasks for this Week	

"The best time to plant a tree was years ago. The second best time is now."

~ Chinese proverb

Big Goal			
This Month's Objective			
Week's Action Step			
	Sunday	Monday	Tuesday
Today's Big Rock			
Priority Tasks			
Daily Tasks			
Daily Bonuses			
NOTES	7	7	7
	8	8	8
	9	9	9
	10	10	10
	11	11	11
	12	12	12
	1	1	1
	2	2	2
	3	3	3
	4	4	4
	5	5	5
	6	6	6
	7	7	7
	8	8	8

Wednesday	Thursday	Friday	Saturday
7	7	7	7
8	8	8	8
9	9	9	9
10	10	10	10
11	11	11	11
12	12	12	12
1	1	1	1
2	2	2	2
3	3	3	3
4	4	4	4
5	5	5	5
6	6	6	6
7	7	7	7
8	8	8	8

Your Weekly ProfitRx

The evidence of my alignment with profit last week was:

This week I appreciate my business because:

This week I choose to feel _____ about my business.

I am trusting my instincts by choosing these inspired actions to do this week:

I trust the Universe to handle everything else I need to attract more profit:

I would be absolutely blown away if this happened this week:

You won't believe it when I tell you what happened in my business. Listen to this:

For the week of	
Big Goal	
This Month's Objective	
This Week's Action Step	
This Week's Big Rocks	
Monday	
Tuesday	
Wednesday	
Thursday	
Friday	
Additional Projects and Tasks for this Week	

"The most difficult thing is the decision to act, the rest is merely tenacity."

~ Amelia Earhart

Big Goal			
This Month's Objective			
Week's Action Step			
	Sunday	**Monday**	**Tuesday**
Today's Big Rock			
Priority Tasks			
Daily Tasks			
Daily Bonuses			
NOTES	7	7	7
	8	8	8
	9	9	9
	10	10	10
	11	11	11
	12	12	12
	1	1	1
	2	2	2
	3	3	3
	4	4	4
	5	5	5
	6	6	6
	7	7	7
	8	8	8

Wednesday	Thursday	Friday	Saturday
7	7	7	7
8	8	8	8
9	9	9	9
10	10	10	10
11	11	11	11
12	12	12	12
1	1	1	1
2	2	2	2
3	3	3	3
4	4	4	4
5	5	5	5
6	6	6	6
7	7	7	7
8	8	8	8

Your Weekly ProfitRx

The evidence of my alignment with profit last week was:

This week I appreciate my business because:

This week I choose to feel _____ about my business.

I am trusting my instincts by choosing these inspired actions to do this week:

I trust the Universe to handle everything else I need to attract more profit:

I would be absolutely blown away if this happened this week:

You won't believe it when I tell you what happened in my business. Listen to this:

For the week of	
Big Goal	
This Month's Objective	
This Week's Action Step	
This Week's Big Rocks	
Monday	
Tuesday	
Wednesday	
Thursday	
Friday	
Additional Projects and Tasks for this Week	

"When everything seems to be going against you, remember that the airplane takes off against the wind, not with it."

~ Henry Ford

	Sunday	Monday	Tuesday
Big Goal			
This Month's Objective			
Week's Action Step			
	Sunday	**Monday**	**Tuesday**
Today's Big Rock			
Priority Tasks			
Daily Tasks			
Daily Bonuses			
NOTES	7	7	7
	8	8	8
	9	9	9
	10	10	10
	11	11	11
	12	12	12
	1	1	1
	2	2	2
	3	3	3
	4	4	4
	5	5	5
	6	6	6
	7	7	7
Big Goal	8	8	8

Wednesday	Thursday	Friday	Saturday
7	7	7	7
8	8	8	8
9	9	9	9
10	10	10	10
11	11	11	11
12	12	12	12
1	1	1	1
2	2	2	2
3	3	3	3
4	4	4	4
5	5	5	5
6	6	6	6
7	7	7	7
8	8	8	8

Your Weekly ProfitRx

The evidence of my alignment with profit last week was:

This week I appreciate my business because:

This week I choose to feel _____ about my business.

I am trusting my instincts by choosing these inspired actions to do this week:

I trust the Universe to handle everything else I need to attract more profit:

I would be absolutely blown away if this happened this week:

You won't believe it when I tell you what happened in my business. Listen to this:

For the week of	
Big Goal	
This Month's Objective	
This Week's Action Step	
This Week's Big Rocks	
Monday	
Tuesday	
Wednesday	
Thursday	
Friday	
Additional Projects and Tasks for this Week	

"I've learned that people will forget what you said, people will forget what you did, but people will never forget how you made them feel."

~ Maya Angelou

Big Goal	
This Month's Objective	
Week's Action Step	

	Sunday	Monday	Tuesday
Today's Big Rock			
Priority Tasks			
Daily Tasks			
Daily Bonuses			
NOTES	7	7	7
	8	8	8
	9	9	9
	10	10	10
	11	11	11
	12	12	12
	1	1	1
	2	2	2
	3	3	3
	4	4	4
	5	5	5
	6	6	6
	7	7	7
Big Goal	8	8	8

Wednesday	Thursday	Friday	Saturday
7	7	7	7
8	8	8	8
9	9	9	9
10	10	10	10
11	11	11	11
12	12	12	12
1	1	1	1
2	2	2	2
3	3	3	3
4	4	4	4
5	5	5	5
6	6	6	6
7	7	7	7
8	8	8	8

Your Weekly ProfitRx

The evidence of my alignment with profit last week was:

This week I appreciate my business because:

This week I choose to feel _____ about my business.

I am trusting my instincts by choosing these inspired actions to do this week:

I trust the Universe to handle everything else I need to attract more profit:

I would be absolutely blown away if this happened this week:

You won't believe it when I tell you what happened in my business. Listen to this:

For the week of	
Big Goal	
This Month's Objective	
This Week's Action Step	
This Week's Big Rocks	
Monday	
Tuesday	
Wednesday	
Thursday	
Friday	
Additional Projects and Tasks for this Week	

"Two roads diverged in a wood, and I,
I took the one less traveled by,
and that has made all the difference."
~ *Robert Frost*

Big Goal			
This Month's Objective			
Week's Action Step			
	Sunday	**Monday**	**Tuesday**
Today's Big Rock			
Priority Tasks			
Daily Tasks			
Daily Bonuses			
NOTES	7	7	7
	8	8	8
	9	9	9
	10	10	10
	11	11	11
	12	12	12
	1	1	1
	2	2	2
	3	3	3
	4	4	4
	5	5	5
	6	6	6
	7	7	7
	8	8	8

Wednesday	Thursday	Friday	Saturday
7	7	7	7
8	8	8	8
9	9	9	9
10	10	10	10
11	11	11	11
12	12	12	12
1	1	1	1
2	2	2	2
3	3	3	3
4	4	4	4
5	5	5	5
6	6	6	6
7	7	7	7
8	8	8	8

Your Weekly ProfitRx

The evidence of my alignment with profit last week was:

This week I appreciate my business because:

This week I choose to feel _____ about my business.

I am trusting my instincts by choosing these inspired actions to do this week:

I trust the Universe to handle everything else I need to attract more profit:

I would be absolutely blown away if this happened this week:

You won't believe it when I tell you what happened in my business. Listen to this:

For the week of	
Big Goal	
This Month's Objective	
This Week's Action Step	
This Week's Big Rocks	
Monday	
Tuesday	
Wednesday	
Thursday	
Friday	
Additional Projects and Tasks for this Week	

"The person who says it cannot be done
should not interrupt
the person who is doing it."

~ Chinese proverb

Big Goal	
This Month's Objective	
Week's Action Step	

	Sunday	Monday	Tuesday
Today's Big Rock			
Priority Tasks			
Daily Tasks			
Daily Bonuses			
NOTES	7	7	7
	8	8	8
	9	9	9
	10	10	10
	11	11	11
	12	12	12
	1	1	1
	2	2	2
	3	3	3
	4	4	4
	5	5	5
	6	6	6
	7	7	7
	8	8	8

Wednesday	Thursday	Friday	Saturday
7	7	7	7
8	8	8	8
9	9	9	9
10	10	10	10
11	11	11	11
12	12	12	12
1	1	1	1
2	2	2	2
3	3	3	3
4	4	4	4
5	5	5	5
6	6	6	6
7	7	7	7
8	8	8	8

Your Weekly ProfitRx

The evidence of my alignment with profit last week was:

This week I appreciate my business because:

This week I choose to feel _____ about my business.

I am trusting my instincts by choosing these inspired actions to do this week:

I trust the Universe to handle everything else I need to attract more profit:

I would be absolutely blown away if this happened this week:

You won't believe it when I tell you what happened in my business. Listen to this:

For the week of	
Big Goal	
This Month's Objective	
This Week's Action Step	
This Week's Big Rocks	
Monday	
Tuesday	
Wednesday	
Thursday	
Friday	
Additional Projects and Tasks for this Week	

> "You miss 100 percent of the shots you don't take."
>
> *~ Wayne Gretzky*

Big Goal				
This Month's Objective				
Week's Action Step				
	Sunday	**Monday**	**Tuesday**	
Today's Big Rock				
Priority Tasks				
Daily Tasks				
Daily Bonuses				
NOTES	7	7	7	
	8	8	8	
	9	9	9	
	10	10	10	
	11	11	11	
	12	12	12	
	1	1	1	
	2	2	2	
	3	3	3	
	4	4	4	
	5	5	5	
	6	6	6	
	7	7	7	
Big Goal	8	8	8	

Wednesday	Thursday	Friday	Saturday
7	7	7	7
8	8	8	8
9	9	9	9
10	10	10	10
11	11	11	11
12	12	12	12
1	1	1	1
2	2	2	2
3	3	3	3
4	4	4	4
5	5	5	5
6	6	6	6
7	7	7	7
8	8	8	8

Well, you have completed the first quarter of your year. How are things going? Take an hour or two to regroup, do a brain dump, organize into Projects with Objectives and Action Items.

Use the space on this and the next page to do your Brain Dump. Feel free to add additional pages if needed.

Project 1:

Objective 1:		
Action Items:	1.	2.
3.	4.	5.
6.	7.	8.

Objective 2:		
Action Items:	1.	2.
3.	4.	5.
6.	7.	8.

Objective 3:		
Action Items:	1.	2.
3.	4.	5.
6.	7.	8.

Objective 4:		
Action Items:	1.	2.
3.	4.	5.
6.	7.	8.

Objective 5:		
Action Items:	1.	2.
3.	4.	5.
6.	7.	8.

Objective 6:		
Action Items:	1.	2.
3.	4.	5.
6.	7.	8.

Project 2:

Objective 1:		
Action Items:	1.	2.
3.	4.	5.
6.	7.	8.

Objective 2:		
Action Items:	1.	2.
3.	4.	5.
6.	7.	8.

Objective 3:		
Action Items:	1.	2.
3.	4.	5.
6.	7.	8.

Objective 4:		
Action Items:	1.	2.
3.	4.	5.
6.	7.	8.

Objective 5:		
Action Items:	1.	2.
3.	4.	5.
6.	7.	8.

Objective 6:		
Action Items:	1.	2.
3.	4.	5.
6.	7.	8.

Project 3:

Objective 1:		
Action Items:	1.	2.
3.	4.	5.
6.	7.	8.

Objective 2:		
Action Items:	1.	2.
3.	4.	5.
6.	7.	8.

Objective 3:		
Action Items:	1.	2.
3.	4.	5.
6.	7.	8.

Objective 4:		
Action Items:	1.	2.
3.	4.	5.
6.	7.	8.

Objective 5:		
Action Items:	1.	2.
3.	4.	5.
6.	7.	8.

Objective 6:		
Action Items:	1.	2.
3.	4.	5.
6.	7.	8.

My Revised Big Goals:

1. **To**

      by

2. **To**

      by

3. **To**

      by

4. **To**

      by

Your Weekly ProfitRx

The evidence of my alignment with profit last week was:

This week I appreciate my business because:

This week I choose to feel _____ about my business.

I am trusting my instincts by choosing these inspired actions to do this week:

I trust the Universe to handle everything else I need to attract more profit:

I would be absolutely blown away if this happened this week:

You won't believe it when I tell you what happened in my business. Listen to this:

For the week of	
Big Goal	
April Objective	
This Week's Action Step	
This Week's Big Rocks	
Monday	
Tuesday	
Wednesday	
Thursday	
Friday	
Additional Projects and Tasks for this Week	

> "The question isn't who is going to let me; it's who is going to stop me."
>
> *~ Ayn Rand*

		Sunday	Monday	Tuesday
Big Goal				
This Month's Objective				
Week's Action Step				
Today's Big Rock				
Priority Tasks				
Daily Tasks				
Daily Bonuses				
NOTES	7	7	7
	8	8	8
	9	9	9
	10	10	10
	11	11	11
	12	12	12
	1	1	1
	2	2	2
	3	3	3
	4	4	4
	5	5	5
	6	6	6
	7	7	7
	8	8	8

Wednesday	Thursday	Friday	Saturday
7	7	7	7
8	8	8	8
9	9	9	9
10	10	10	10
11	11	11	11
12	12	12	12
1	1	1	1
2	2	2	2
3	3	3	3
4	4	4	4
5	5	5	5
6	6	6	6
7	7	7	7
8	8	8	8

Your Weekly ProfitRx

The evidence of my alignment with profit last week was:

This week I appreciate my business because:

This week I choose to feel _____ about my business.

I am trusting my instincts by choosing these inspired actions to do this week:

I trust the Universe to handle everything else I need to attract more profit:

I would be absolutely blown away if this happened this week:

You won't believe it when I tell you what happened in my business. Listen to this:

For the week of	
Big Goal	
This Month's Objective	
This Week's Action Step	
This Week's Big Rocks	
Monday	
Tuesday	
Wednesday	
Thursday	
Friday	
Additional Projects and Tasks for this Week	

"Everything you've ever wanted is on the other side of fear."

~ George Addair

Big Goal			
This Month's Objective			
Week's Action Step			
	Sunday	Monday	Tuesday
Today's Big Rock			
Priority Tasks			
Daily Tasks			
Daily Bonuses			
NOTES	7	7	7
	8	8	8
	9	9	9
	10	10	10
	11	11	11
	12	12	12
	1	1	1
	2	2	2
	3	3	3
	4	4	4
	5	5	5
	6	6	6
	7	7	7
	8	8	8

Wednesday	Thursday	Friday	Saturday
7	7	7	7
8	8	8	8
9	9	9	9
10	10	10	10
11	11	11	11
12	12	12	12
1	1	1	1
2	2	2	2
3	3	3	3
4	4	4	4
5	5	5	5
6	6	6	6
7	7	7	7
8	8	8	8

Your Weekly ProfitRx

The evidence of my alignment with profit last week was:

This week I appreciate my business because:

This week I choose to feel _____ about my business.

I am trusting my instincts by choosing these inspired actions to do this week:

I trust the Universe to handle everything else I need to attract more profit:

I would be absolutely blown away if this happened this week:

You won't believe it when I tell you what happened in my business. Listen to this:

For the week of	
Big Goal	
April Objective	
This Week's Action Step	
This Week's Big Rocks	
Monday	
Tuesday	
Wednesday	
Thursday	
Friday	
Additional Projects and Tasks for this Week	

"Rarely have I seen a situation where doing less than the other guy is a good strategy."

~ Jimmy Spithill

		Sunday	Monday	Tuesday
Big Goal				
This Month's Objective				
Week's Action Step				
Today's Big Rock				
Priority Tasks				
Daily Tasks				
Daily Bonuses				
NOTES		7	7	7
		8	8	8
		9	9	9
		10	10	10
		11	11	11
		12	12	12
		1	1	1
		2	2	2
		3	3	3
		4	4	4
		5	5	5
		6	6	6
		7	7	7
		8	8	8

Wednesday	Thursday	Friday	Saturday
7	7	7	7
8	8	8	8
9	9	9	9
10	10	10	10
11	11	11	11
12	12	12	12
1	1	1	1
2	2	2	2
3	3	3	3
4	4	4	4
5	5	5	5
6	6	6	6
7	7	7	7
8	8	8	8

Your Weekly ProfitRx

The evidence of my alignment with profit last week was:

This week I appreciate my business because:

This week I choose to feel _____ about my business.

I am trusting my instincts by choosing these inspired actions to do this week:

I trust the Universe to handle everything else I need to attract more profit:

I would be absolutely blown away if this happened this week:

You won't believe it when I tell you what happened in my business. Listen to this:

For the week of	
Big Goal	
This Month's Objective	
This Week's Action Step	
This Week's Big Rocks	
Monday	
Tuesday	
Wednesday	
Thursday	
Friday	
Additional Projects and Tasks for this Week	

"Twenty years from now, you will be more disappointed by the things that you didn't do than by the ones you did do, so throw off the bowlines, sail away from safe harbor, catch the trade winds in your sails. Explore, Dream, Discover."

~ *Mark Twain*

	Sunday	Monday	Tuesday
Big Goal			
This Month's Objective			
Week's Action Step			
	Sunday	**Monday**	**Tuesday**
Today's Big Rock			
Priority Tasks			
Daily Tasks			
Daily Bonuses			
NOTES	7	7	7
	8	8	8
	9	9	9
	10	10	10
	11	11	11
	12	12	12
	1	1	1
	2	2	2
	3	3	3
	4	4	4
	5	5	5
	6	6	6
	7	7	7
	8	8	8

Wednesday	Thursday	Friday	Saturday
7	7	7	7
8	8	8	8
9	9	9	9
10	10	10	10
11	11	11	11
12	12	12	12
1	1	1	1
2	2	2	2
3	3	3	3
4	4	4	4
5	5	5	5
6	6	6	6
7	7	7	7
8	8	8	8

Your Weekly ProfitRx

The evidence of my alignment with profit last week was:

This week I appreciate my business because:

This week I choose to feel _____ about my business.

I am trusting my instincts by choosing these inspired actions to do this week:

I trust the Universe to handle everything else I need to attract more profit:

I would be absolutely blown away if this happened this week:

You won't believe it when I tell you what happened in my business. Listen to this:

For the week of	
Big Goal	
This Month's Objective	
This Week's Action Step	
This Week's Big Rocks	
Monday	
Tuesday	
Wednesday	
Thursday	
Friday	
Additional Projects and Tasks for this Week	

"The greater danger for most of us lies not in setting our aim too high and falling short, but in setting our aim too low and achieving our mark."

~ Michelangelo

	Sunday	Monday	Tuesday
Big Goal			
This Month's Objective			
Week's Action Step			
Today's Big Rock			
Priority Tasks			
Daily Tasks			
Daily Bonuses			
NOTES	7	7	7
	8	8	8
	9	9	9
	10	10	10
	11	11	11
	12	12	12
	1	1	1
	2	2	2
	3	3	3
	4	4	4
	5	5	5
	6	6	6
	7	7	7
	8	8	8

Wednesday	Thursday	Friday	Saturday
7	7	7	7
8	8	8	8
9	9	9	9
10	10	10	10
11	11	11	11
12	12	12	12
1	1	1	1
2	2	2	2
3	3	3	3
4	4	4	4
5	5	5	5
6	6	6	6
7	7	7	7
8	8	8	8

Your Weekly ProfitRx

The evidence of my alignment with profit last week was:

This week I appreciate my business because:

This week I choose to feel _____ about my business.

I am trusting my instincts by choosing these inspired actions to do this week:

I trust the Universe to handle everything else I need to attract more profit:

I would be absolutely blown away if this happened this week:

You won't believe it when I tell you what happened in my business. Listen to this:

For the week of	
Big Goal	
This Month's Objective	
This Week's Action Step	
This Week's Big Rocks	
Monday	
Tuesday	
Wednesday	
Thursday	
Friday	
Additional Projects and Tasks for this Week	

"Waiting for perfect is never as smart as making progress."

~ Seth Godin

	Sunday	Monday	Tuesday
Big Goal			
This Month's Objective			
Week's Action Step			
	Sunday	**Monday**	**Tuesday**
Today's Big Rock			
Priority Tasks			
Daily Tasks			
Daily Bonuses			
NOTES	7	7	7
	8	8	8
	9	9	9
	10	10	10
	11	11	11
	12	12	12
	1	1	1
	2	2	2
	3	3	3
	4	4	4
	5	5	5
	6	6	6
	7	7	7
Big Goal	8	8	8

Wednesday	Thursday	Friday	Saturday
7	7	7	7
8	8	8	8
9	9	9	9
10	10	10	10
11	11	11	11
12	12	12	12
1	1	1	1
2	2	2	2
3	3	3	3
4	4	4	4
5	5	5	5
6	6	6	6
7	7	7	7
8	8	8	8

Your Weekly ProfitRx

The evidence of my alignment with profit last week was:

This week I appreciate my business because:

This week I choose to feel _____ about my business.

I am trusting my instincts by choosing these inspired actions to do this week:

I trust the Universe to handle everything else I need to attract more profit:

I would be absolutely blown away if this happened this week:

You won't believe it when I tell you what happened in my business. Listen to this:

For the week of	
Big Goal	
This Month's Objective	
This Week's Action Step	
This Week's Big Rocks	
Monday	
Tuesday	
Wednesday	
Thursday	
Friday	
Additional Projects and Tasks for this Week	

> "A leader is one who knows the way, goes the way, and shows the way."
>
> *~ John Maxwell*

	Sunday	Monday	Tuesday
Big Goal			
This Month's Objective			
Week's Action Step			
	Sunday	**Monday**	**Tuesday**
Today's Big Rock			
Priority Tasks			
Daily Tasks			
Daily Bonuses			
NOTES	7	7	7
	8	8	8
	9	9	9
	10	10	10
	11	11	11
	12	12	12
	1	1	1
	2	2	2
	3	3	3
	4	4	4
	5	5	5
	6	6	6
	7	7	7
	8	8	8

Wednesday	Thursday	Friday	Saturday
7	7	7	7
8	8	8	8
9	9	9	9
10	10	10	10
11	11	11	11
12	12	12	12
1	1	1	1
2	2	2	2
3	3	3	3
4	4	4	4
5	5	5	5
6	6	6	6
7	7	7	7
8	8	8	8

Your Weekly ProfitRx

The evidence of my alignment with profit last week was:

This week I appreciate my business because:

This week I choose to feel _____ about my business.

I am trusting my instincts by choosing these inspired actions to do this week:

I trust the Universe to handle everything else I need to attract more profit:

I would be absolutely blown away if this happened this week:

You won't believe it when I tell you what happened in my business. Listen to this:

For the week of	
Big Goal	
This Month's Objective	
This Week's Action Step	
This Week's Big Rocks	
Monday	
Tuesday	
Wednesday	
Thursday	
Friday	
Additional Projects and Tasks for this Week	

"Goals aren't enough. You need goals plus deadlines: goals big enough to get excited about and deadlines to make you run. One isn't much good without the other, but together they can be tremendous."

~ Ben Feldman

Big Goal			
This Month's Objective			
Week's Action Step			
	Sunday	**Monday**	**Tuesday**
Today's Big Rock			
Priority Tasks			
Daily Tasks			
Daily Bonuses			
NOTES	7	7	7
	8	8	8
	9	9	9
	10	10	10
	11	11	11
	12	12	12
	1	1	1
	2	2	2
	3	3	3
	4	4	4
	5	5	5
	6	6	6
	7	7	7
Big Goal	8	8	8

Wednesday	Thursday	Friday	Saturday
7	7	7	7
8	8	8	8
9	9	9	9
10	10	10	10
11	11	11	11
12	12	12	12
1	1	1	1
2	2	2	2
3	3	3	3
4	4	4	4
5	5	5	5
6	6	6	6
7	7	7	7
8	8	8	8

Your Weekly ProfitRx

The evidence of my alignment with profit last week was:

This week I appreciate my business because:

This week I choose to feel _____ about my business.

I am trusting my instincts by choosing these inspired actions to do this week:

I trust the Universe to handle everything else I need to attract more profit:

I would be absolutely blown away if this happened this week:

You won't believe it when I tell you what happened in my business. Listen to this:

For the week of	
Big Goal	
This Month's Objective	
This Week's Action Step	
This Week's Big Rocks	
Monday	
Tuesday	
Wednesday	
Thursday	
Friday	
Additional Projects and Tasks for this Week	

"Be so good they can't ignore you."

~ Steve Martin

Big Goal			
This Month's Objective			
Week's Action Step			
	Sunday	Monday	Tuesday
Today's Big Rock			
Priority Tasks			
Daily Tasks			
Daily Bonuses			
NOTES	7	7	7
	8	8	8
	9	9	9
	10	10	10
	11	11	11
	12	12	12
	1	1	1
	2	2	2
	3	3	3
	4	4	4
	5	5	5
	6	6	6
	7	7	7
	8	8	8

Wednesday	Thursday	Friday	Saturday
7	7	7	7
8	8	8	8
9	9	9	9
10	10	10	10
11	11	11	11
12	12	12	12
1	1	1	1
2	2	2	2
3	3	3	3
4	4	4	4
5	5	5	5
6	6	6	6
7	7	7	7
8	8	8	8

Your Weekly ProfitRx

The evidence of my alignment with profit last week was:

This week I appreciate my business because:

This week I choose to feel _____ about my business.

I am trusting my instincts by choosing these inspired actions to do this week:

I trust the Universe to handle everything else I need to attract more profit:

I would be absolutely blown away if this happened this week:

You won't believe it when I tell you what happened in my business. Listen to this:

For the week of	
Big Goal	
This Month's Objective	
This Week's Action Step	
This Week's Big Rocks	
Monday	
Tuesday	
Wednesday	
Thursday	
Friday	
Additional Projects and Tasks for this Week	

> "Leaders think and talk about the solutions.
> Followers think and talk about the problems."
> ~ *Brian Tracy*

	Sunday	Monday	Tuesday
Big Goal			
This Month's Objective			
Week's Action Step			
	Sunday	**Monday**	**Tuesday**
Today's Big Rock			
Priority Tasks			
Daily Tasks			
Daily Bonuses			
NOTES	7	7	7
	8	8	8
	9	9	9
	10	10	10
	11	11	11
	12	12	12
	1	1	1
	2	2	2
	3	3	3
	4	4	4
	5	5	5
	6	6	6
	7	7	7
Big Goal	8	8	8

Wednesday	Thursday	Friday	Saturday
7	7	7	7
8	8	8	8
9	9	9	9
10	10	10	10
11	11	11	11
12	12	12	12
1	1	1	1
2	2	2	2
3	3	3	3
4	4	4	4
5	5	5	5
6	6	6	6
7	7	7	7
8	8	8	8

Your Weekly ProfitRx

The evidence of my alignment with profit last week was:

This week I appreciate my business because:

This week I choose to feel _____ about my business.

I am trusting my instincts by choosing these inspired actions to do this week:

I trust the Universe to handle everything else I need to attract more profit:

I would be absolutely blown away if this happened this week:

You won't believe it when I tell you what happened in my business. Listen to this:

For the week of	
Big Goal	
This Month's Objective	
This Week's Action Step	
This Week's Big Rocks	
Monday	
Tuesday	
Wednesday	
Thursday	
Friday	
Additional Projects and Tasks for this Week	

> "There are no secrets to success. It is the result of preparation, hard work, and learning from failure."
> ~ *Colin Powell*

Big Goal			
This Month's Objective			
Week's Action Step			
	Sunday	**Monday**	**Tuesday**
Today's Big Rock			
Priority Tasks			
Daily Tasks			
Daily Bonuses			
NOTES	7	7	7
	8	8	8
	9	9	9
	10	10	10
	11	11	11
	12	12	12
	1	1	1
	2	2	2
	3	3	3
	4	4	4
	5	5	5
	6	6	6
	7	7	7
	8	8	8

Wednesday	Thursday	Friday	Saturday
7	7	7	7
8	8	8	8
9	9	9	9
10	10	10	10
11	11	11	11
12	12	12	12
1	1	1	1
2	2	2	2
3	3	3	3
4	4	4	4
5	5	5	5
6	6	6	6
7	7	7	7
8	8	8	8

Your Weekly ProfitRx

The evidence of my alignment with profit last week was:

This week I appreciate my business because:

This week I choose to feel _____ about my business.

I am trusting my instincts by choosing these inspired actions to do this week:

I trust the Universe to handle everything else I need to attract more profit:

I would be absolutely blown away if this happened this week:

You won't believe it when I tell you what happened in my business. Listen to this:

For the week of	
Big Goal	
This Month's Objective	
This Week's Action Step	
This Week's Big Rocks	
Monday	
Tuesday	
Wednesday	
Thursday	
Friday	
Additional Projects and Tasks for this Week	

"Don't worry about failure; you only have to be right once."

~ Drew Houston

Big Goal			
This Month's Objective			
Week's Action Step			
	Sunday	**Monday**	**Tuesday**
Today's Big Rock			
Priority Tasks			
Daily Tasks			
Daily Bonuses			
NOTES	7	7	7
	8	8	8
	9	9	9
	10	10	10
	11	11	11
	12	12	12
	1	1	1
	2	2	2
	3	3	3
	4	4	4
	5	5	5
	6	6	6
	7	7	7
	8	8	8

Wednesday	Thursday	Friday	Saturday
7	7	7	7
8	8	8	8
9	9	9	9
10	10	10	10
11	11	11	11
12	12	12	12
1	1	1	1
2	2	2	2
3	3	3	3
4	4	4	4
5	5	5	5
6	6	6	6
7	7	7	7
8	8	8	8

Your Weekly ProfitRx

The evidence of my alignment with profit last week was:

This week I appreciate my business because:

This week I choose to feel _____ about my business.

I am trusting my instincts by choosing these inspired actions to do this week:

I trust the Universe to handle everything else I need to attract more profit:

I would be absolutely blown away if this happened this week:

You won't believe it when I tell you what happened in my business. Listen to this:

For the week of	
Big Goal	
This Month's Objective	
This Week's Action Step	
This Week's Big Rocks	
Monday	
Tuesday	
Wednesday	
Thursday	
Friday	
Additional Projects and Tasks for this Week	

"I knew that if I failed I wouldn't regret that, but I knew the one thing I might regret is not trying."

~ Jeff Bezos

		Sunday	Monday	Tuesday
Big Goal				
This Month's Objective				
Week's Action Step				
Today's Big Rock				
Priority Tasks				
Daily Tasks				
Daily Bonuses				
NOTES		7	7	7
		8	8	8
		9	9	9
		10	10	10
		11	11	11
		12	12	12
		1	1	1
		2	2	2
		3	3	3
		4	4	4
		5	5	5
		6	6	6
		7	7	7
		8	8	8

Wednesday	Thursday	Friday	Saturday
7	7	7	7
8	8	8	8
9	9	9	9
10	10	10	10
11	11	11	11
12	12	12	12
1	1	1	1
2	2	2	2
3	3	3	3
4	4	4	4
5	5	5	5
6	6	6	6
7	7	7	7
8	8	8	8

Well, you have completed the second quarter of your year. How are things going? It is time to evaluate where you are and where you are headed. Take an hour or two to regroup, do a brain dump, organize into Projects with Objectives and Action Items.

Use the space on this and the next page to do your Brain Dump. Feel free to add additional pages if needed.

Project 1:

Objective 1:		
Action Items:	1.	2.
3.	4.	5.
6.	7.	8.

Objective 2:		
Action Items:	1.	2.
3.	4.	5.
6.	7.	8.

Objective 3:		
Action Items:	1.	2.
3.	4.	5.
6.	7.	8.

Objective 4:		
Action Items:	1.	2.
3.	4.	5.
6.	7.	8.

Objective 5:		
Action Items:	1.	2.
3.	4.	5.
6.	7.	8.

Objective 6:		
Action Items:	1.	2.
3.	4.	5.
6.	7.	8.

Project 2:

Objective 1:		
Action Items:	1.	2.
3.	4.	5.
6.	7.	8.

Objective 2:		
Action Items:	1.	2.
3.	4.	5.
6.	7.	8.

Objective 3:		
Action Items:	1.	2.
3.	4.	5.
6.	7.	8.

Objective 4:		
Action Items:	1.	2.
3.	4.	5.
6.	7.	8.

Objective 5:		
Action Items:	1.	2.
3.	4.	5.
6.	7.	8.

Objective 6:		
Action Items:	1.	2.
3.	4.	5.
6.	7.	8.

Project 3:

Objective 1:		
Action Items:	1.	2.
3.	4.	5.
6.	7.	8.

Objective 2:		
Action Items:	1.	2.
3.	4.	5.
6.	7.	8.

Objective 3:		
Action Items:	1.	2.
3.	4.	5.
6.	7.	8.

Objective 4:		
Action Items:	1.	2.
3.	4.	5.
6.	7.	8.

Objective 5:		
Action Items:	1.	2.
3.	4.	5.
6.	7.	8.

Objective 6:		
Action Items:	1.	2.
3.	4.	5.
6.	7.	8.

My Revised Big Goals:

1. **To**

    by

2. **To**

    by

3. **To**

    by

4. **To**

    by

Your Weekly ProfitRx

The evidence of my alignment with profit last week was:

This week I appreciate my business because:

This week I choose to feel _____ about my business.

I am trusting my instincts by choosing these inspired actions to do this week:

I trust the Universe to handle everything else I need to attract more profit:

I would be absolutely blown away if this happened this week:

You won't believe it when I tell you what happened in my business. Listen to this:

For the week of	
Big Goal	
This Month's Objective	
This Week's Action Step	
This Week's Big Rocks	
Monday	
Tuesday	
Wednesday	
Thursday	
Friday	
Additional Projects and Tasks for this Week	

> "A pessimist sees the difficulty in every opportunity; an optimist sees the opportunity in every difficulty."
> ~ *Winston Churchill*

	Sunday	Monday	Tuesday
Big Goal			
This Month's Objective			
Week's Action Step			
	Sunday	**Monday**	**Tuesday**
Today's Big Rock			
Priority Tasks			
Daily Tasks			
Daily Bonuses			
NOTES	7	7	7
	8	8	8
	9	9	9
	10	10	10
	11	11	11
	12	12	12
	1	1	1
	2	2	2
	3	3	3
	4	4	4
	5	5	5
	6	6	6
	7	7	7
	8	8	8

Wednesday	Thursday	Friday	Saturday
7	7	7	7
8	8	8	8
9	9	9	9
10	10	10	10
11	11	11	11
12	12	12	12
1	1	1	1
2	2	2	2
3	3	3	3
4	4	4	4
5	5	5	5
6	6	6	6
7	7	7	7
8	8	8	8

Your Weekly ProfitRx

The evidence of my alignment with profit last week was:

This week I appreciate my business because:

This week I choose to feel _____ about my business.

I am trusting my instincts by choosing these inspired actions to do this week:

I trust the Universe to handle everything else I need to attract more profit:

I would be absolutely blown away if this happened this week:

You won't believe it when I tell you what happened in my business. Listen to this:

For the week of	
Big Goal	
This Month's Objective	
This Week's Action Step	
This Week's Big Rocks	
Monday	
Tuesday	
Wednesday	
Thursday	
Friday	
Additional Projects and Tasks for this Week	

> "As long as you're going to be thinking anyway, think big."
>
> ~ *Donald Trump*

		Sunday	Monday	Tuesday
Big Goal				
This Month's Objective				
Week's Action Step				
Today's Big Rock				
Priority Tasks				
Daily Tasks				
Daily Bonuses				
NOTES		7	7	7
		8	8	8
		9	9	9
		10	10	10
		11	11	11
		12	12	12
		1	1	1
		2	2	2
		3	3	3
		4	4	4
		5	5	5
		6	6	6
		7	7	7
		8	8	8

Wednesday	Thursday	Friday	Saturday
7	7	7	7
8	8	8	8
9	9	9	9
10	10	10	10
11	11	11	11
12	12	12	12
1	1	1	1
2	2	2	2
3	3	3	3
4	4	4	4
5	5	5	5
6	6	6	6
7	7	7	7
8	8	8	8

Your Weekly ProfitRx

The evidence of my alignment with profit last week was:

This week I appreciate my business because:

This week I choose to feel _____ about my business.

I am trusting my instincts by choosing these inspired actions to do this week:

I trust the Universe to handle everything else I need to attract more profit:

I would be absolutely blown away if this happened this week:

You won't believe it when I tell you what happened in my business. Listen to this:

For the week of	
Big Goal	
This Month's Objective	
This Week's Action Step	
This Week's Big Rocks	
Monday	
Tuesday	
Wednesday	
Thursday	
Friday	
Additional Projects and Tasks for this Week	

"Whether you think you can,
or think you can't — you're right."
~ Henry Ford

Big Goal			
This Month's Objective			
Week's Action Step			
	Sunday	Monday	Tuesday
Today's Big Rock			
Priority Tasks			
Daily Tasks			
Daily Bonuses			
NOTES	7	7	7
	8	8	8
	9	9	9
	10	10	10
	11	11	11
	12	12	12
	1	1	1
	2	2	2
	3	3	3
	4	4	4
	5	5	5
	6	6	6
	7	7	7
	8	8	8

Wednesday	Thursday	Friday	Saturday
7	7	7	7
8	8	8	8
9	9	9	9
10	10	10	10
11	11	11	11
12	12	12	12
1	1	1	1
2	2	2	2
3	3	3	3
4	4	4	4
5	5	5	5
6	6	6	6
7	7	7	7
8	8	8	8

Your Weekly ProfitRx

The evidence of my alignment with profit last week was:

This week I appreciate my business because:

This week I choose to feel _____ about my business.

I am trusting my instincts by choosing these inspired actions to do this week:

I trust the Universe to handle everything else I need to attract more profit:

I would be absolutely blown away if this happened this week:

You won't believe it when I tell you what happened in my business. Listen to this:

For the week of	
Big Goal	
This Month's Objective	
This Week's Action Step	
This Week's Big Rocks	
Monday	
Tuesday	
Wednesday	
Thursday	
Friday	
Additional Projects and Tasks for this Week	

"You don't learn to walk by following rules. You learn by doing and falling over."
~ Richard Branson

	Sunday	Monday	Tuesday
Big Goal			
This Month's Objective			
Week's Action Step			
Today's Big Rock			
Priority Tasks			
Daily Tasks			
Daily Bonuses			
NOTES	7	7	7
	8	8	8
	9	9	9
	10	10	10
	11	11	11
	12	12	12
	1	1	1
	2	2	2
	3	3	3
	4	4	4
	5	5	5
	6	6	6
	7	7	7
Big Goal	8	8	8

Wednesday	Thursday	Friday	Saturday
7	7	7	7
8	8	8	8
9	9	9	9
10	10	10	10
11	11	11	11
12	12	12	12
1	1	1	1
2	2	2	2
3	3	3	3
4	4	4	4
5	5	5	5
6	6	6	6
7	7	7	7
8	8	8	8

Your Weekly ProfitRx

The evidence of my alignment with profit last week was:

This week I appreciate my business because:

This week I choose to feel _____ about my business.

I am trusting my instincts by choosing these inspired actions to do this week:

I trust the Universe to handle everything else I need to attract more profit:

I would be absolutely blown away if this happened this week:

You won't believe it when I tell you what happened in my business. Listen to this:

For the week of	
Big Goal	
This Month's Objective	
This Week's Action Step	
This Week's Big Rocks	
Monday	
Tuesday	
Wednesday	
Thursday	
Friday	
Additional Projects and Tasks for this Week	

"Your most unhappy customers are your greatest source of learning."
~ Bill Gates

	Sunday	Monday	Tuesday
Big Goal			
This Month's Objective			
Week's Action Step			
Today's Big Rock			
Priority Tasks			
Daily Tasks			
Daily Bonuses			
NOTES	7	7	7
	8	8	8
	9	9	9
	10	10	10
	11	11	11
	12	12	12
	1	1	1
	2	2	2
	3	3	3
	4	4	4
	5	5	5
	6	6	6
	7	7	7
	8	8	8

Wednesday	Thursday	Friday	Saturday
7	7	7	7
8	8	8	8
9	9	9	9
10	10	10	10
11	11	11	11
12	12	12	12
1	1	1	1
2	2	2	2
3	3	3	3
4	4	4	4
5	5	5	5
6	6	6	6
7	7	7	7
8	8	8	8

Your Weekly ProfitRx

The evidence of my alignment with profit last week was:

This week I appreciate my business because:

This week I choose to feel _____ about my business.

I am trusting my instincts by choosing these inspired actions to do this week:

I trust the Universe to handle everything else I need to attract more profit:

I would be absolutely blown away if this happened this week:

You won't believe it when I tell you what happened in my business. Listen to this:

For the week of	
Big Goal	
This Month's Objective	
This Week's Action Step	
This Week's Big Rocks	
Monday	
Tuesday	
Wednesday	
Thursday	
Friday	
Additional Projects and Tasks for this Week	

"Always treat your employees exactly as you want them to treat your best customers."
~ Stephen R. Covey

Big Goal			
This Month's Objective			
Week's Action Step			
	Sunday	**Monday**	**Tuesday**
Today's Big Rock			
Priority Tasks			
Daily Tasks			
Daily Bonuses			
NOTES	7	7	7
	8	8	8
	9	9	9
	10	10	10
	11	11	11
	12	12	12
	1	1	1
	2	2	2
	3	3	3
	4	4	4
	5	5	5
	6	6	6
	7	7	7
	8	8	8

Wednesday	Thursday	Friday	Saturday
7	7	7	7
8	8	8	8
9	9	9	9
10	10	10	10
11	11	11	11
12	12	12	12
1	1	1	1
2	2	2	2
3	3	3	3
4	4	4	4
5	5	5	5
6	6	6	6
7	7	7	7
8	8	8	8

Your Weekly ProfitRx

The evidence of my alignment with profit last week was:

This week I appreciate my business because:

This week I choose to feel _____ about my business.

I am trusting my instincts by choosing these inspired actions to do this week:

I trust the Universe to handle everything else I need to attract more profit:

I would be absolutely blown away if this happened this week:

You won't believe it when I tell you what happened in my business. Listen to this:

For the week of	
Big Goal	
This Month's Objective	
This Week's Action Step	
This Week's Big Rocks	
Monday	
Tuesday	
Wednesday	
Thursday	
Friday	
Additional Projects and Tasks for this Week	

> "When you find an idea that you just can't stop thinking about,
> that's probably a good one to pursue."
> *~ Josh James*

Big Goal			
This Month's Objective			
Week's Action Step			
	Sunday	**Monday**	**Tuesday**
Today's Big Rock			
Priority Tasks			
Daily Tasks			
Daily Bonuses			
NOTES	7	7	7
	8	8	8
	9	9	9
	10	10	10
	11	11	11
	12	12	12
	1	1	1
	2	2	2
	3	3	3
	4	4	4
	5	5	5
	6	6	6
	7	7	7
	8	8	8

Wednesday	Thursday	Friday	Saturday
7	7	7	7
8	8	8	8
9	9	9	9
10	10	10	10
11	11	11	11
12	12	12	12
1	1	1	1
2	2	2	2
3	3	3	3
4	4	4	4
5	5	5	5
6	6	6	6
7	7	7	7
8	8	8	8

Your Weekly ProfitRx

The evidence of my alignment with profit last week was:

This week I appreciate my business because:

This week I choose to feel _____ about my business.

I am trusting my instincts by choosing these inspired actions to do this week:

I trust the Universe to handle everything else I need to attract more profit:

I would be absolutely blown away if this happened this week:

You won't believe it when I tell you what happened in my business. Listen to this:

For the week of	
Big Goal	
This Month's Objective	
This Week's Action Step	
This Week's Big Rocks	
Monday	
Tuesday	
Wednesday	
Thursday	
Friday	
Additional Projects and Tasks for this Week	

"Never, never, never give up."
~ Winston Churchill

		Sunday	Monday	Tuesday
Big Goal				
This Month's Objective				
Week's Action Step				
Today's Big Rock				
Priority Tasks				
Daily Tasks				
Daily Bonuses				
NOTES		7	7	7
		8	8	8
		9	9	9
		10	10	10
		11	11	11
		12	12	12
		1	1	1
		2	2	2
		3	3	3
		4	4	4
		5	5	5
		6	6	6
		7	7	7
Big Goal		8	8	8

	Wednesday	Thursday	Friday	Saturday
7	7	7	7	7
8	8	8	8	8
9	9	9	9	9
10	10	10	10	10
11	11	11	11	11
12	12	12	12	12
1	1	1	1	1
2	2	2	2	2
3	3	3	3	3
4	4	4	4	4
5	5	5	5	5
6	6	6	6	6
7	7	7	7	7
8	8	8	8	8

Your Weekly ProfitRx

The evidence of my alignment with profit last week was:

This week I appreciate my business because:

This week I choose to feel _____ about my business.

I am trusting my instincts by choosing these inspired actions to do this week:

I trust the Universe to handle everything else I need to attract more profit:

I would be absolutely blown away if this happened this week:

You won't believe it when I tell you what happened in my business. Listen to this:

For the week of	
Big Goal	
This Month's Objective	
This Week's Action Step	
This Week's Big Rocks	
Monday	
Tuesday	
Wednesday	
Thursday	
Friday	
Additional Projects and Tasks for this Week	

"We must all suffer one of two things: the pain of discipline or the pain of regret."
~ Jim Rohn

Big Goal			
This Month's Objective			
Week's Action Step			
	Sunday	Monday	Tuesday
Today's Big Rock			
Priority Tasks			
Daily Tasks			
Daily Bonuses			
NOTES	7	7	7
	8	8	8
	9	9	9
	10	10	10
	11	11	11
	12	12	12
	1	1	1
	2	2	2
	3	3	3
	4	4	4
	5	5	5
	6	6	6
	7	7	7
Big Goal	8	8	8

Wednesday	Thursday	Friday	Saturday
7	7	7	7
8	8	8	8
9	9	9	9
10	10	10	10
11	11	11	11
12	12	12	12
1	1	1	1
2	2	2	2
3	3	3	3
4	4	4	4
5	5	5	5
6	6	6	6
7	7	7	7
8	8	8	8

Your Weekly ProfitRx

The evidence of my alignment with profit last week was:

This week I appreciate my business because:

This week I choose to feel _____ about my business.

I am trusting my instincts by choosing these inspired actions to do this week:

I trust the Universe to handle everything else I need to attract more profit:

I would be absolutely blown away if this happened this week:

You won't believe it when I tell you what happened in my business. Listen to this:

For the week of	
Big Goal	
September Objective	
This Week's Action Step	
This Week's Big Rocks	
Monday	
Tuesday	
Wednesday	
Thursday	
Friday	
Additional Projects and Tasks for this Week	

> "Achievement seems to be connected with action. Successful men and women keep moving. They make mistakes but they don't quit."
>
> ~ *Conrad Hilton*

Big Goal			
This Month's Objective			
Week's Action Step			
	Sunday	**Monday**	**Tuesday**
Today's Big Rock			
Priority Tasks			
Daily Tasks			
Daily Bonuses			
+NOTES	7	7	7
	8	8	8
	9	9	9
	10	10	10
	11	11	11
	12	12	12
	1	1	1
	2	2	2
	3	3	3
	4	4	4
	5	5	5
	6	6	6
	7	7	7
Big Goal	8	8	8

Wednesday	Thursday	Friday	Saturday
7	7	7	7
8	8	8	8
9	9	9	9
10	10	10	10
11	11	11	11
12	12	12	12
1	1	1	1
2	2	2	2
3	3	3	3
4	4	4	4
5	5	5	5
6	6	6	6
7	7	7	7
8	8	8	8

Your Weekly ProfitRx

The evidence of my alignment with profit last week was:

This week I appreciate my business because:

This week I choose to feel _____ about my business.

I am trusting my instincts by choosing these inspired actions to do this week:

I trust the Universe to handle everything else I need to attract more profit:

I would be absolutely blown away if this happened this week:

You won't believe it when I tell you what happened in my business. Listen to this:

For the week of	
Big Goal	
September Objective	
This Week's Action Step	
This Week's Big Rocks	
Monday	
Tuesday	
Wednesday	
Thursday	
Friday	
Additional Projects and Tasks for this Week	

"There's a difference between interest and commitment. When you're interested in doing something, you do it only when it's convenient. When you're committed to something, you accept no excuses - only results."
~ *Ken Blanchard*

Big Goal			
This Month's Objective			
Week's Action Step			
	Sunday	Monday	Tuesday
Today's Big Rock			
Priority Tasks			
Daily Tasks			
Daily Bonuses			
NOTES	7	7	7
	8	8	8
	9	9	9
	10	10	10
	11	11	11
	12	12	12
	1	1	1
	2	2	2
	3	3	3
	4	4	4
	5	5	5
	6	6	6
	7	7	7
Big Goal	8	8	8

	Wednesday	Thursday	Friday	Saturday
7				
8				
9				
10				
11				
12				
1				
2				
3				
4				
5				
6				
7				
8				

Your Weekly ProfitRx

The evidence of my alignment with profit last week was:

This week I appreciate my business because:

This week I choose to feel _____ about my business.

I am trusting my instincts by choosing these inspired actions to do this week:

I trust the Universe to handle everything else I need to attract more profit:

I would be absolutely blown away if this happened this week:

You won't believe it when I tell you what happened in my business. Listen to this:

For the week of	
Big Goal	
September Objective	
This Week's Action Step	
This Week's Big Rocks	
Monday	
Tuesday	
Wednesday	
Thursday	
Friday	
Additional Projects and Tasks for this Week	

"Success is not final, failure is not fatal: it is the courage to continue that counts."
~ Winston Churchill

Big Goal				
This Month's Objective				
Week's Action Step				
	Sunday		Monday	Tuesday
Today's Big Rock				
Priority Tasks				
Daily Tasks				
Daily Bonuses				
NOTES	7		7	7
	8		8	8
	9		9	9
	10		10	10
	11		11	11
	12		12	12
	1		1	1
	2		2	2
	3		3	3
	4		4	4
	5		5	5
	6		6	6
	7		7	7
	8		8	8

Wednesday	Thursday	Friday	Saturday
7	7	7	7
8	8	8	8
9	9	9	9
10	10	10	10
11	11	11	11
12	12	12	12
1	1	1	1
2	2	2	2
3	3	3	3
4	4	4	4
5	5	5	5
6	6	6	6
7	7	7	7
8	8	8	8

Your Weekly ProfitRx

The evidence of my alignment with profit last week was:

This week I appreciate my business because:

This week I choose to feel _____ about my business.

I am trusting my instincts by choosing these inspired actions to do this week:

I trust the Universe to handle everything else I need to attract more profit:

I would be absolutely blown away if this happened this week:

You won't believe it when I tell you what happened in my business. Listen to this:

For the week of	
Big Goal	
September Objective	
This Week's Action Step	
This Week's Big Rocks	
Monday	
Tuesday	
Wednesday	
Thursday	
Friday	
Additional Projects and Tasks for this Week	

"Change is inevitable,

Growth is optional"

~ *John Maxwell*

Big Goal	
This Month's Objective	
Week's Action Step	

	Sunday	Monday	Tuesday
Today's Big Rock			
Priority Tasks			
Daily Tasks			
Daily Bonuses			
NOTES	7	7	7
	8	8	8
	9	9	9
	10	10	10
	11	11	11
	12	12	12
	1	1	1
	2	2	2
	3	3	3
	4	4	4
	5	5	5
	6	6	6
	7	7	7
Big Goal	8	8	8

Wednesday	Thursday	Friday	Saturday
7	7	7	7
8	8	8	8
9	9	9	9
10	10	10	10
11	11	11	11
12	12	12	12
1	1	1	1
2	2	2	2
3	3	3	3
4	4	4	4
5	5	5	5
6	6	6	6
7	7	7	7
8	8	8	8

Well, you have completed the third quarter of your year. How are things going? It is time to evaluate where you are and where you are headed. Take an hour or two to regroup, do a brain dump, organize into Projects with Objectives and Action Items. Now is a great time to start planning for next year. Have you updated your Business and Marketing Plans, created a budget and new sales forecast. Get in touch if you need help with these at info@kisstrategies.ca.

Project 1:

Objective 1:		
Action Items:	1.	2.
3.	4.	5.
6.	7.	8.

Objective 2:		
Action Items:	1.	2.
3.	4.	5.
6.	7.	8.

Objective 3:		
Action Items:	1.	2.
3.	4.	5.
6.	7.	8.

Objective 4:		
Action Items:	1.	2.
3.	4.	5.
6.	7.	8.

Objective 5:		
Action Items:	1.	2.
3.	4.	5.
6.	7.	8.

Objective 6:		
Action Items:	1.	2.
3.	4.	5.
6.	7.	8.

Project 2:

Objective 1:		
Action Items:	1.	2.
3.	4.	5.
6.	7.	8.

Objective 2:		
Action Items:	1.	2.
3.	4.	5.
6.	7.	8.

Objective 3:		
Action Items:	1.	2.
3.	4.	5.
6.	7.	8.

Objective 4:		
Action Items:	1.	2.
3.	4.	5.
6.	7.	8.

Objective 5:		
Action Items:	1.	2.
3.	4.	5.
6.	7.	8.

Objective 6:		
Action Items:	1.	2.
3.	4.	5.
6.	7.	8.

Project 3:

Objective 1:		
Action Items:	1.	2.
3.	4.	5.
6.	7.	8.

Objective 2:		
Action Items:	1.	2.
3.	4.	5.
6.	7.	8.

Objective 3:		
Action Items:	1.	2.
3.	4.	5.
6.	7.	8.

Objective 4:		
Action Items:	1.	2.
3.	4.	5.
6.	7.	8.

Objective 5:		
Action Items:	1.	2.
3.	4.	5.
6.	7.	8.

Objective 6:		
Action Items:	1.	2.
3.	4.	5.
6.	7.	8.

My Revised Big Goals:

1. **To**

   by

2. **To**

   by

3. **To**

   by

4. **To**

   by

Your Weekly ProfitRx

The evidence of my alignment with profit last week was:

This week I appreciate my business because:

This week I choose to feel _____ about my business.

I am trusting my instincts by choosing these inspired actions to do this week:

I trust the Universe to handle everything else I need to attract more profit:

I would be absolutely blown away if this happened this week:

You won't believe it when I tell you what happened in my business. Listen to this:

For the week of	
Big Goal	
This Month's Objective	
This Week's Action Step	
This Week's Big Rocks	
Monday	
Tuesday	
Wednesday	
Thursday	
Friday	
Additional Projects and Tasks for this Week	

"Luck is what happens when preparation meets opportunity"
~ *Seneca*

Big Goal				
This Month's Objective				
Week's Action Step				
	Sunday	Monday	Tuesday	
Today's Big Rock				
Priority Tasks				
Daily Tasks				
Daily Bonuses				
NOTES	7	7	7	
	8	8	8	
	9	9	9	
	10	10	10	
	11	11	11	
	12	12	12	
	1	1	1	
	2	2	2	
	3	3	3	
	4	4	4	
	5	5	5	
	6	6	6	
	7	7	7	
Big Goal	8	8	8	

Wednesday	Thursday	Friday	Saturday
7	7	7	7
8	8	8	8
9	9	9	9
10	10	10	10
11	11	11	11
12	12	12	12
1	1	1	1
2	2	2	2
3	3	3	3
4	4	4	4
5	5	5	5
6	6	6	6
7	7	7	7
8	8	8	8

Your Weekly ProfitRx

The evidence of my alignment with profit last week was:

This week I appreciate my business because:

This week I choose to feel _____ about my business.

I am trusting my instincts by choosing these inspired actions to do this week:

I trust the Universe to handle everything else I need to attract more profit:

I would be absolutely blown away if this happened this week:

You won't believe it when I tell you what happened in my business. Listen to this:

For the week of	
Big Goal	
This Month's Objective	
This Week's Action Step	
This Week's Big Rocks	
Monday	
Tuesday	
Wednesday	
Thursday	
Friday	
Additional Projects and Tasks for this Week	

> "Insanity: doing the same thing over and over again and expecting different results."
> ~ *Albert Einstein*

Big Goal				
This Month's Objective				
Week's Action Step				
	Sunday	**Monday**	**Tuesday**	
Today's Big Rock				
Priority Tasks				
Daily Tasks				
Daily Bonuses				
NOTES	7	7	7	
	8	8	8	
	9	9	9	
	10	10	10	
	11	11	11	
	12	12	12	
	1	1	1	
	2	2	2	
	3	3	3	
	4	4	4	
	5	5	5	
	6	6	6	
	7	7	7	
Big Goal	8	8	8	

Wednesday	Thursday	Friday	Saturday
7	7	7	7
8	8	8	8
9	9	9	9
10	10	10	10
11	11	11	11
12	12	12	12
1	1	1	1
2	2	2	2
3	3	3	3
4	4	4	4
5	5	5	5
6	6	6	6
7	7	7	7
8	8	8	8

Your Weekly ProfitRx

The evidence of my alignment with profit last week was:

This week I appreciate my business because:

This week I choose to feel _____ about my business.

I am trusting my instincts by choosing these inspired actions to do this week:

I trust the Universe to handle everything else I need to attract more profit:

I would be absolutely blown away if this happened this week:

You won't believe it when I tell you what happened in my business. Listen to this:

For the week of	
Big Goal	
This Month's Objective	
This Week's Action Step	
This Week's Big Rocks	
Monday	
Tuesday	
Wednesday	
Thursday	
Friday	
Additional Projects and Tasks for this Week	

> *"You must be the change you wish to see in the world."*
> *~ Mahatma Gandhi*

	Sunday	Monday	Tuesday
Big Goal			
This Month's Objective			
Week's Action Step			
Today's Big Rock			
Priority Tasks			
Daily Tasks			
Daily Bonuses			
NOTES	7	7	7
	8	8	8
	9	9	9
	10	10	10
	11	11	11
	12	12	12
	1	1	1
	2	2	2
	3	3	3
	4	4	4
	5	5	5
	6	6	6
	7	7	7
	8	8	8

Wednesday	Thursday	Friday	Saturday
7	7	7	7
8	8	8	8
9	9	9	9
10	10	10	10
11	11	11	11
12	12	12	12
1	1	1	1
2	2	2	2
3	3	3	3
4	4	4	4
5	5	5	5
6	6	6	6
7	7	7	7
8	8	8	8

Your Weekly ProfitRx

The evidence of my alignment with profit last week was:

This week I appreciate my business because:

This week I choose to feel _____ about my business.

I am trusting my instincts by choosing these inspired actions to do this week:

I trust the Universe to handle everything else I need to attract more profit:

I would be absolutely blown away if this happened this week:

You won't believe it when I tell you what happened in my business. Listen to this:

For the week of	
Big Goal	
October Objective	
This Week's Action Step	
This Week's Big Rocks	
Monday	
Tuesday	
Wednesday	
Thursday	
Friday	
Additional Projects and Tasks for this Week	

We cannot solve our problems with the same thinking we used when we created them.
~ Albert Einstein

	Sunday	Monday	Tuesday
Big Goal			
This Month's Objective			
Week's Action Step			
	Sunday	Monday	Tuesday
Today's Big Rock			
Priority Tasks			
Daily Tasks			
Daily Bonuses			
NOTES	7	7	7
	8	8	8
	9	9	9
	10	10	10
	11	11	11
	12	12	12
	1	1	1
	2	2	2
	3	3	3
	4	4	4
	5	5	5
	6	6	6
	7	7	7
Big Goal	8	8	8

Wednesday	Thursday	Friday	Saturday
7	7	7	7
8	8	8	8
9	9	9	9
10	10	10	10
11	11	11	11
12	12	12	12
1	1	1	1
2	2	2	2
3	3	3	3
4	4	4	4
5	5	5	5
6	6	6	6
7	7	7	7
8	8	8	8

Your Weekly ProfitRx

The evidence of my alignment with profit last week was:

This week I appreciate my business because:

This week I choose to feel _____ about my business.

I am trusting my instincts by choosing these inspired actions to do this week:

I trust the Universe to handle everything else I need to attract more profit:

I would be absolutely blown away if this happened this week:

You won't believe it when I tell you what happened in my business. Listen to this:

For the week of	
Big Goal	
November Objective	
This Week's Action Step	
This Week's Big Rocks	
Monday	
Tuesday	
Wednesday	
Thursday	
Friday	
Additional Projects and Tasks for this Week	

> "The mind is everything.
> What you think you become."
> ~ Buddha

Big Goal	
This Month's Objective	
Week's Action Step	

	Sunday	Monday	Tuesday
Today's Big Rock			
Priority Tasks			
Daily Tasks			
Daily Bonuses			
NOTES	7	7	7
	8	8	8
	9	9	9
	10	10	10
	11	11	11
	12	12	12
	1	1	1
	2	2	2
	3	3	3
	4	4	4
	5	5	5
	6	6	6
	7	7	7
Big Goal	8	8	8

Wednesday	Thursday	Friday	Saturday
7	7	7	7
8	8	8	8
9	9	9	9
10	10	10	10
11	11	11	11
12	12	12	12
1	1	1	1
2	2	2	2
3	3	3	3
4	4	4	4
5	5	5	5
6	6	6	6
7	7	7	7
8	8	8	8

Your Weekly ProfitRx

The evidence of my alignment with profit last week was:

This week I appreciate my business because:

This week I choose to feel _____ about my business.

I am trusting my instincts by choosing these inspired actions to do this week:

I trust the Universe to handle everything else I need to attract more profit:

I would be absolutely blown away if this happened this week:

You won't believe it when I tell you what happened in my business. Listen to this:

For the week of	
Big Goal	
This Month's Objective	
This Week's Action Step	
This Week's Big Rocks	
Monday	
Tuesday	
Wednesday	
Thursday	
Friday	
Additional Projects and Tasks for this Week	

> "What you focus on expands. So focus on what you want, not what you do not want."
> ~Esther Jno-Charles

Big Goal	
This Month's Objective	
Week's Action Step	

	Sunday	Monday	Tuesday
Today's Big Rock			
Priority Tasks			
Daily Tasks			
Daily Bonuses			
NOTES	7	7	7
	8	8	8
	9	9	9
	10	10	10
	11	11	11
	12	12	12
	1	1	1
	2	2	2
	3	3	3
	4	4	4
	5	5	5
	6	6	6
	7	7	7
	8	8	8

Wednesday	Thursday	Friday	Saturday
7	7	7	7
8	8	8	8
9	9	9	9
10	10	10	10
11	11	11	11
12	12	12	12
1	1	1	1
2	2	2	2
3	3	3	3
4	4	4	4
5	5	5	5
6	6	6	6
7	7	7	7
8	8	8	8

Your Weekly ProfitRx

The evidence of my alignment with profit last week was:

This week I appreciate my business because:

This week I choose to feel _____ about my business.

I am trusting my instincts by choosing these inspired actions to do this week:

I trust the Universe to handle everything else I need to attract more profit:

I would be absolutely blown away if this happened this week:

You won't believe it when I tell you what happened in my business. Listen to this:

For the week of	
Big Goal	
This Month's Objective	
This Week's Action Step	
This Week's Big Rocks	
Monday	
Tuesday	
Wednesday	
Thursday	
Friday	
Additional Projects and Tasks for this Week	

"I may not have gone where I intended to go, but I think I have ended up where I needed to be."
~ Douglas Adams

	Sunday	Monday	Tuesday
Big Goal			
This Month's Objective			
Week's Action Step			
Today's Big Rock			
Priority Tasks			
Daily Tasks			
Daily Bonuses			
NOTES	7	7	7
	8	8	8
	9	9	9
	10	10	10
	11	11	11
	12	12	12
	1	1	1
	2	2	2
	3	3	3
	4	4	4
	5	5	5
	6	6	6
	7	7	7
	8	8	8

Wednesday	Thursday	Friday	Saturday
7	7	7	7
8	8	8	8
9	9	9	9
10	10	10	10
11	11	11	11
12	12	12	12
1	1	1	1
2	2	2	2
3	3	3	3
4	4	4	4
5	5	5	5
6	6	6	6
7	7	7	7
8	8	8	8

Your Weekly ProfitRx

The evidence of my alignment with profit last week was:

This week I appreciate my business because:

This week I choose to feel _____ about my business.

I am trusting my instincts by choosing these inspired actions to do this week:

I trust the Universe to handle everything else I need to attract more profit:

I would be absolutely blown away if this happened this week:

You won't believe it when I tell you what happened in my business. Listen to this:

For the week of	
Big Goal	
This Month's Objective	
This Week's Action Step	
This Week's Big Rocks	
Monday	
Tuesday	
Wednesday	
Thursday	
Friday	
Additional Projects and Tasks for this Week	

"Do, or do not. There is no try."
~ *Yoda*

	Sunday	Monday	Tuesday
Big Goal			
This Month's Objective			
Week's Action Step			
	Sunday	**Monday**	**Tuesday**
Today's Big Rock			
Priority Tasks			
Daily Tasks			
Daily Bonuses			
NOTES	7	7	7
	8	8	8
	9	9	9
	10	10	10
	11	11	11
	12	12	12
	1	1	1
	2	2	2
	3	3	3
	4	4	4
	5	5	5
	6	6	6
	7	7	7
Big Goal	8	8	8

Wednesday	Thursday	Friday	Saturday
7	7	7	7
8	8	8	8
9	9	9	9
10	10	10	10
11	11	11	11
12	12	12	12
1	1	1	1
2	2	2	2
3	3	3	3
4	4	4	4
5	5	5	5
6	6	6	6
7	7	7	7
8	8	8	8

Your Weekly ProfitRx

The evidence of my alignment with profit last week was:

This week I appreciate my business because:

This week I choose to feel _____ about my business.

I am trusting my instincts by choosing these inspired actions to do this week:

I trust the Universe to handle everything else I need to attract more profit:

I would be absolutely blown away if this happened this week:

You won't believe it when I tell you what happened in my business. Listen to this:

For the week of	
Big Goal	
November Objective	
This Week's Action Step	
This Week's Big Rocks	
Monday	
Tuesday	
Wednesday	
Thursday	
Friday	
Additional Projects and Tasks for this Week	

"That which does not kill us makes us stronger."
~ Friedrich Nietzsche

Big Goal			
This Month's Objective			
Week's Action Step			
	Sunday	**Monday**	**Tuesday**
Today's Big Rock			
Priority Tasks			
Daily Tasks			
Daily Bonuses			
NOTES	7	7	7
	8	8	8
	9	9	9
	10	10	10
	11	11	11
	12	12	12
	1	1	1
	2	2	2
	3	3	3
	4	4	4
	5	5	5
	6	6	6
	7	7	7
Big Goal	8	8	8

Wednesday	Thursday	Friday	Saturday
7	7	7	7
8	8	8	8
9	9	9	9
10	10	10	10
11	11	11	11
12	12	12	12
1	1	1	1
2	2	2	2
3	3	3	3
4	4	4	4
5	5	5	5
6	6	6	6
7	7	7	7
8	8	8	8

Your Weekly ProfitRx

The evidence of my alignment with profit last week was:

This week I appreciate my business because:

This week I choose to feel _____ about my business.

I am trusting my instincts by choosing these inspired actions to do this week:

I trust the Universe to handle everything else I need to attract more profit:

I would be absolutely blown away if this happened this week:

You won't believe it when I tell you what happened in my business. Listen to this:

For the week of	
Big Goal	
December Objective	
This Week's Action Step	
This Week's Big Rocks	
Monday	
Tuesday	
Wednesday	
Thursday	
Friday	
Additional Projects and Tasks for this Week	

"Life is like riding a bicycle. To keep your balance, you must keep moving."
~ Albert Einstein

		Sunday	Monday	Tuesday
Big Goal				
This Month's Objective				
Week's Action Step				
Today's Big Rock				
Priority Tasks				
Daily Tasks				
Daily Bonuses				
NOTES		7	7	7
		8	8	8
		9	9	9
		10	10	10
		11	11	11
		12	12	12
		1	1	1
		2	2	2
		3	3	3
		4	4	4
		5	5	5
		6	6	6
		7	7	7
		8	8	8

Wednesday	Thursday	Friday	Saturday
7	7	7	7
8	8	8	8
9	9	9	9
10	10	10	10
11	11	11	11
12	12	12	12
1	1	1	1
2	2	2	2
3	3	3	3
4	4	4	4
5	5	5	5
6	6	6	6
7	7	7	7
8	8	8	8

Your Weekly ProfitRx

The evidence of my alignment with profit last week was:

This week I appreciate my business because:

This week I choose to feel _____ about my business.

I am trusting my instincts by choosing these inspired actions to do this week:

I trust the Universe to handle everything else I need to attract more profit:

I would be absolutely blown away if this happened this week:

You won't believe it when I tell you what happened in my business. Listen to this:

For the week of	
Big Goal	
This Month's Objective	
This Week's Action Step	
This Week's Big Rocks	
Monday	
Tuesday	
Wednesday	
Thursday	
Friday	
Additional Projects and Tasks for this Week	

"Do one thing every day that scares you."
~ *Eleanor Roosevelt*

	Sunday	Monday	Tuesday
Big Goal			
This Month's Objective			
Week's Action Step			
	Sunday	**Monday**	**Tuesday**
Today's Big Rock			
Priority Tasks			
Daily Tasks			
Daily Bonuses			
NOTES	7	7	7
	8	8	8
	9	9	9
	10	10	10
	11	11	11
	12	12	12
	1	1	1
	2	2	2
	3	3	3
	4	4	4
	5	5	5
	6	6	6
	7	7	7
Big Goal	8	8	8

Wednesday	Thursday	Friday	Saturday
7	7	7	7
8	8	8	8
9	9	9	9
10	10	10	10
11	11	11	11
12	12	12	12
1	1	1	1
2	2	2	2
3	3	3	3
4	4	4	4
5	5	5	5
6	6	6	6
7	7	7	7
8	8	8	8

Your Weekly ProfitRx

The evidence of my alignment with profit last week was:

This week I appreciate my business because:

This week I choose to feel _____ about my business.

I am trusting my instincts by choosing these inspired actions to do this week:

I trust the Universe to handle everything else I need to attract more profit:

I would be absolutely blown away if this happened this week:

You won't believe it when I tell you what happened in my business. Listen to this:

For the week of	
Big Goal	
December Objective	
This Week's Action Step	
This Week's Big Rocks	
Monday	
Tuesday	
Wednesday	
Thursday	
Friday	
Additional Projects and Tasks for this Week	

"Our deepest fear is not that we are inadequate. Our deepest fear is that we are powerful beyond measure."
~ Marianne Williamson

	Sunday	Monday	Tuesday
Big Goal			
This Month's Objective			
Week's Action Step			
	Sunday	**Monday**	**Tuesday**
Today's Big Rock			
Priority Tasks			
Daily Tasks			
Daily Bonuses			
NOTES	7	7	7
	8	8	8
	9	9	9
	10	10	10
	11	11	11
	12	12	12
	1	1	1
	2	2	2
	3	3	3
	4	4	4
	5	5	5
	6	6	6
	7	7	7
Big Goal	8	8	8

Wednesday	Thursday	Friday	Saturday
7	7	7	7
8	8	8	8
9	9	9	9
10	10	10	10
11	11	11	11
12	12	12	12
1	1	1	1
2	2	2	2
3	3	3	3
4	4	4	4
5	5	5	5
6	6	6	6
7	7	7	7
8	8	8	8

Your Weekly ProfitRx

The evidence of my alignment with profit last week was:

This week I appreciate my business because:

This week I choose to feel _____ about my business.

I am trusting my instincts by choosing these inspired actions to do this week:

I trust the Universe to handle everything else I need to attract more profit:

I would be absolutely blown away if this happened this week:

You won't believe it when I tell you what happened in my business. Listen to this:

For the week of	
Big Goal	
This Month's Objective	
This Week's Action Step	
This Week's Big Rocks	
Monday	
Tuesday	
Wednesday	
Thursday	
Friday	
Additional Projects and Tasks for this Week	

> "You have brains in your head.
> You have feet in your shoes.
> You can steer yourself any direction you choose."
> ~ *Dr. Suess*

Big Goal			
This Month's Objective			
Week's Action Step			
	Sunday	Monday	Tuesday
Today's Big Rock			
Priority Tasks			
Daily Tasks			
Daily Bonuses			
NOTES	7	7	7
	8	8	8
	9	9	9
	10	10	10
	11	11	11
	12	12	12
	1	1	1
	2	2	2
	3	3	3
	4	4	4
	5	5	5
	6	6	6
	7	7	7
	8	8	8

Wednesday	Thursday	Friday	Saturday
7	7	7	7
8	8	8	8
9	9	9	9
10	10	10	10
11	11	11	11
12	12	12	12
1	1	1	1
2	2	2	2
3	3	3	3
4	4	4	4
5	5	5	5
6	6	6	6
7	7	7	7
8	8	8	8

Your Weekly ProfitRx

The evidence of my alignment with profit last week was:

This week I appreciate my business because:

This week I choose to feel _____ about my business.

I am trusting my instincts by choosing these inspired actions to do this week:

I trust the Universe to handle everything else I need to attract more profit:

I would be absolutely blown away if this happened this week:

You won't believe it when I tell you what happened in my business. Listen to this:

For the week of	
Big Goal	
This Month's Objective	
This Week's Action Step	
This Week's Big Rocks	
Monday	
Tuesday	
Wednesday	
Thursday	
Friday	
Additional Projects and Tasks for this Week	

We hope you have had an action packed, profitable year and wish you the same in !
Cheers!

	Sunday	Monday	Tuesday
Big Goal			
This Month's Objective			
Week's Action Step			
Today's Big Rock			
Priority Tasks			
Daily Tasks			
Daily Bonuses			
NOTES	7	7	7
	8	8	8
	9	9	9
	10	10	10
	11	11	11
	12	12	12
	1	1	1
	2	2	2
	3	3	3
	4	4	4
	5	5	5
	6	6	6
	7	7	7
	8	8	8

Wednesday	Thursday	Friday	Saturday
7	7	7	7
8	8	8	8
9	9	9	9
10	10	10	10
11	11	11	11
12	12	12	12
1	1	1	1
2	2	2	2
3	3	3	3
4	4	4	4
5	5	5	5
6	6	6	6
7	7	7	7
8	8	8	8